DISCIPLING WOMEN

BY LORI JOINER

crupress

Published by: Cru Press
100 Lake Hart Drive 2500
Orlando, FL 32832
www.crupress.com

ISBN-13: 978-1-57334-077-9

Cover design by Traci Yau
Cover photo by Jelani Memory Photography - iStockphoto
Inside design by Brian L. Byers
Typeset in Adobe® Caslon Pro & Myriad Pro

This book is designed to provide accurate and authoritative information in regard to the subject
matter covered. It is sold with the understanding that neither the author nor the publisher is
engaged in rendering legal, counseling, or any other professional services. If legal advice or other
professional advice, including counseling, is required, the services of a competent professional
person should be sought. The author and publisher specifically disclaim any and all liability arising
directly or indirectly from the use or application of any information contained in this book. Some
of the anecdotal illustrations in this book are true to life and are included with the permission of
the persons involved. All other illustrations are composites of real situations, and any resemblance
of people living or dead is coincidental.

Unless otherwise identified, all Scripture quotations in this publication are taken from the Holy
Bible, New International Version (NIV), Copyright 1973, 1978, 1984 by International Bible Society. Used by permission of Zondervan. All rights reserved.

Library of Congress Cataloging-in-Publication Data

Joiner, Lori, 1972-

Discipling Women / Lori Joiner.

p. cm.

Includes bibliographical references.

ISBN-13: 978-1-57334-077-9
Library of Congress Control Number: 2012943864

1. Women—Growth 2. Religious aspects—Christianity

Printed in the United States of America

1 2 3 4 5 6 7 8 / 15 14 13 12 11

ACKNOWLEDGEMENTS

Thank you, Wayne and Karen Copelin, for letting me live with you during the bulk of writing this book. Thank you for taking me into your home during quite a transition time in my life, and for your incredible feedback on my manuscript and my different speaking engagements. My time spent in your home and with your family touched me forever.

Thank you to my own past disciplers and mentors who challenged me through the years and left a lasting, godly mark upon my life: Schuyler and Karen Pratt, who led me to Christ in high school; Rhonda Haralson and Christi Allen, my college disciplers; and Shannon Compere, my wonderful regional director for 10 years. I treasure the investment you made in me.

Thank you to the women I have had the privilege and honor to disciple through the years, and thank you for letting me share your stories.

Kay Tuel, for your example of discipling a city's worth of women while raising four children, and for introducing me to some of the amazing women represented in these pages.

Cheri Gillis, my best friend in life — if not for your life, many of these chapters would not be here. I love you, B!

Thank you to my parents, Don Fleener and Gerre Keller — both your lives have helped mold me into who I am today, and I am so thankful you are my mom and dad. And to my dear sister, Renee Fleener, who has walked with me through not only the twists and turns of this book, but those in life as well.

Thank you to my wonderful husband, Alan, who said while we were dating, "I want to take care of you so you can continue to do all the things you do for God." He has provided a wonderful home for me and our two precious sons, Josh and Jake.

Thank you to my editors, Paul Schwarz and Daniela Byers, for helping make this book much better than I could.

And most of all, I thank the Lord. If not for His grace, His rescuing me out of the miry clay, and His setting my feet on solid ground, I would have nothing to offer anyone. I am so grateful for the life He has given me and I seek to make Him proud. Oh, Lord, will I ever grasp your timing?

 PREFACE

What a thrill to help another woman put her faith in Christ and see her grow into a godly, mature, Spirit-filled woman of God. My life has been changed for the better because of other women pouring themselves into my life — encouraging me, challenging me, pressing me forward, holding me accountable, and loving me. By God's grace He has seen fit to allow me to have this role in other women's lives as well.

Whether it be discipling women when I was a college student living on a dorm floor at the University of North Texas or while a staff member with Campus Crusade for Christ, from women in my church to women from the gym to women I have met while doing laundry, I love being a part of women's lives and being available for God to use as his tool where he sees fit.

In these pages I have written about my experiences, what has worked for me, and what I have seen to be easily transferable. It is my hope that these stories and resources will help women who want to disciple other women. I tried to keep women in many stages of life in mind, but I realize that not every chapter will be useful to every woman in every situation. I do trust that most women will find some things that will give them confidence to move forward to help another woman grow closer to the Lord.

It is my vision to help lead women to Christ, disciple them in God's Word, and help them grow closer to Jesus Christ — even when I am very old, perhaps living in a nursing home! I never want it to stop!

Contents

PART I : FROM THE BEGINNING

PART II : ISSUES WOMEN FACE

CONTENTS

PART III : COMMONLY ASKED QUESTIONS

 **PART I**

From the Beginning

Introduction

When I arrived at Christi's home, she greeted me warmly with a big smile, and I settled onto her couch next to my best friend, Cheri. We had both signed up to be in a Bible study during our junior year of college, and this was our first meeting. The group of about ten women talked freely about the Bible lesson Christi had prepared for us while we munched on snacks she had prepared for us.

While this Bible study was a wonderful place to grow in my relationship with the Lord, the real transformation happened in my one-on-one times with Christi. To see her interactions with her children, husband, and me were wonderful, powerful models of a Christian home. I remember her telling me stories about her missionary adventures in Kenya, and I determined I wanted to go on a mission trip somewhere overseas. I told her about how I wanted to share Christ with the women on my dorm floor, and she taught me, saying, "Lori, these are the questions college students are asking, so these are the verses you should memorize, and I will teach you an easy way to explain the gospel." I also talked with her about my struggles with my boyfriend at the time, and she lovingly walked me through that season.

Above all, Christi invested time in me. She let me into her life, taught me the Bible, and challenged me to share what I knew with others at college and around the world. Christi made a real difference in my life, and in the lives of plenty of other women, and I longed to be that type of loving, caring person in another woman's life.

Whether you are new to discipleship or have been discipling women for years, Part 1 will help give you some tracks to run on and perhaps some new ideas to use in your discipleship relationships. From what to talk about during discipleship times to fun things to do with your disciple, from material to teach your disciple to how to have difficult conversations with her, I desire for you to find encouragement in your discipleship endeavors.

Okay, let's get started!

 **CHAPTER 1**

A Biblical Perspective on Discipleship

I greeted Samantha as she walked in the door. She'd made an appointment to meet with me during a missions conference in Florida at which I'd spoken. She was a pretty girl with curly, dark brown hair and a bright smile. We sat on my couch and began to talk about the conference, the weather, and where she was from.

As I curled my legs up on the couch, she explained to me why she wanted to see me. "I can't stop cutting myself," Samantha said, her chin quivering. "I hate it, but when I get depressed or down about how I look, I just give in again."

I could see the scars on one of her arms, about 10 thin red whelps of differing lengths. I have to say it was a struggle not to let my jaw hit the floor. Even though I'd heard of this habit before, I would've never guessed that this sweet girl who sat with me on my couch, was struggling with this. We talked at length about the issue, spent time in prayer, and even shed a few tears.

"Samantha," I advised her, "it is so important for you to talk regularly with someone in your life back home. You've already told me you want to grow in your relationship with God and make a difference for Him. You need to get into a discipleship relationship."

"A what?" Samantha asked.

"A discipleship relationship," I said again.

"What is that?"

Samantha had put her faith in Christ years before, but she had never been discipled. Even though she could rely on Christ for everything, no one had walked with her and helped her mature spiritually. After I explained what discipleship was, she was excited at the prospect of an older woman who would disciple her in her walk with God.

As she walked out the door I couldn't help but wonder how her life might have been different had someone discipled her through the years. Perhaps if someone had taught her the lesson of Psalm 139 that she is wonderfully made by God, she would not have struggled with such low self-esteem. Perhaps if someone had taught her years ago that her body is the temple of the Holy Spirit, she never would have begun the habit of cutting herself. Perhaps if someone had taught her how to walk intimately with God, she could have gone to Him with her struggles instead of taking them out on herself. Perhaps …

The good news is that Samantha is still relatively young. She has her whole life ahead of her. She can make it, be discipled, and begin to walk with God in a whole new way. Unfortunately, though, the old scars will always be there.

There are thousands of Samanthas who need a woman to come alongside to love them, care for them, and encourage them in their walk with God. You and I have the ability to be that loving discipler in their lives. We don't have to have all the answers; we don't have to be the "perfect" Christian. We need only be willing to be used by God to embrace another woman in the holy endeavor of discipleship.

What is Discipleship?

Discipleship is a ministry whereby a more mature believer builds an intentional relationship with a less mature believer (relatively new to the faith, or saved but with little to no growth) for the purpose of teaching the content of the gospel and demonstrating the Christian lifestyle.

What it's not

* Professional counseling in which a person might need medication

* Mentorship or a Big Brother/Big Sister program- although some things may overlap

* Pedantic dissemination of facts, which is mere academia or a transfer of knowledge

* Evangelism

* Picking someone up for church every Sunday

What it is

- Intentional
- A goal-oriented objective toward which the discipler aims. Discipler seeks to accomplish something specific in the life of another. Goals are measurable. One measure may be the evolving of the disciple into a discipler.
- Teaching characteristics of faith such as holiness, righteousness, and eternal perspective.
- Teaching disciplines of faith such as witnessing, tithing, and missions.
- A spiritual endeavor of investing, teaching, and encouraging another person toward Christ and others.

More than just a weekly appointment, discipleship is a life rub-off. It's spending time together and walking through life together, because certain life lessons are more caught than taught.

For example, one day I was at a Lowe's home improvement store with Amanda, a woman I discipled. As we got our paint mixed, I began talking about Jesus to the employee attending us. We had a great conversation, and I was able to tell him that God loved him and desired a personal relationship with him. Of all the lessons I taught Amanda during our weekly discipleship time what she remembered most were the lessons she caught when we were simply following Christ together.

Why Disciple?

Old Testament

In the Old Testament, "discipleship" was at the heart of Jewish faith. It was a function of the family under the father's leadership and, following the captivity, a function also of the synagogue. Fathers were instructed to teach their children the Law of Moses — how to honor and please the Lord, and how to follow His commandments:

> "And these words which I command you today shall be in your heart. You shall teach them diligently to your children, and shall talk of them when you sit in your house, when you walk by the way, when you lie down, and when you rise up" (Deuteronomy 6:6,7; NKJV).

In instructing Aaron and his sons in their priestly duties, God said, "You must teach the Israelites all the decrees the Lord has given them through Moses" (Leviticus 10:8-11, NASB).

In Jesus' day, the family and the synagogue remained the central forum for learning and teaching the principles of the community of faith. Until the final year of His ministry, which Bible scholars call "the year of opposition," Jesus regularly taught in the synagogues: "He went to Nazareth, where he had been brought up, and on the Sabbath day he went into the synagogue, as was his custom" (Luke 4:16, NIV).

New Testament

Jesus made the invitation to be a learner personal when he asked certain individuals to follow Him. The "following" implied an ongoing (discipling) process. Jesus wanted men to follow Him — not just to be saved, but also to learn how to teach and equip others. We see this in his invitation to Peter and Andrew:

> "As Jesus was walking beside the Sea of Galilee, he saw two brothers, Simon called Peter and his brother Andrew. They were casting a net into the lake, for they were fishermen. 'Come follow me', Jesus said, 'and I will make you fishers of men.' At once they left their nets and followed him" (Matthew 4:18-20, NIV).

Jesus invited twelve men to accompany him on a three-year journey. During that time they were disciples and learners. In that process their characters were transformed.

In the Book of Acts, there are many pictures of discipleship. On Paul's second missionary journey he returned to towns where he had preached the gospel on the first journey. His purpose was to strengthen and encourage the believers, and at Lystra he met a disciple named Timothy. Always seeking those whom he could disciple, and with a disciple already with him (Silas), Paul took Timothy along for the rest of the journey (Acts 16:1-5, NIV). It's interesting to note that the more mature believers like Paul and Barnabas took younger and presumably less mature men like Silas and John Mark with them when they ministered (Acts 15: 36-41, NIV).

In fact, on each of Paul's missionary journeys, he brought along a younger believer or group of believers with him (Acts 13:5, 15:40, 16:3, 20:4). He did this not out of fear or loneliness, but rather to make the most of every opportunity to teach others: "And the things you have heard me say in the presence of many witness, entrust to reliable men who will also be qualified to teach others" (2 Timothy 2:2, NIV). Paul charges Timothy to teach others that which he has learned from Paul.

There is the expectation that Timothy will pass on what he has learned to his own disciples, and we are expected to do likewise.

Paul addresses women specifically in Titus 2:3 when he says:

> "Likewise, teach the older women to be reverent in the way they live, not to be slanderers or addicted to too much wine, but to teach what is good. Then they can train the younger women to love their husbands and children, to be self-controlled and pure, to be busy at home, to be kind, and to be subject to their husbands, so that no one will malign the word of God" (NIV).

Again, Paul is emphasizing the importance of passing on to others what we have learned.

Acts 29

Luke completed the 28 chapters we now know as the Book of Acts in 68 A.D. Today, you and I are writing the 29th chapter, just as Christians have been doing since the first century. Christianity is one generation from extinction, meaning that if we as believers don't pass on what we know about the Lord and a relationship with Him to the next generation, that generation will have nothing to pass on to the one after. The dynamic that stands between Christianity and its extinction is the degree to which Christians take seriously the mantle of discipling others:

> "All authority in heaven and on earth has been given to me. Therefore go and make disciples of all nations, baptizing them in the name of the Father and of the Son and of the Holy Spirit, and teaching them to obey everything I have commanded you. And

surely I am with you always, to the end of the age" (Matthew 28:18-20, NIV).

This verse convicts me. It states that disciple-making is not an option, not merely a good suggestion, not just something to do when you have accomplished all your other goals in life. It is a mandate. We are, in the power of the Holy Spirit, to tell others the good news of Jesus Christ and to make disciples. Whatever we've learned up to this point about God and His Word, we are to teach to others.

Evangelism and Discipleship

The Bible exhorts us to evangelize and to make disciples. It's important to understand the differences between these two tasks.

"To evangelize" is to proclaim the good news of Jesus Christ. This biblical concept is expressed through the Greek verb evangelizo. Evangelism can be thought of as an event. It is proclaiming the good news, whereby a person hears the gospel and responds in faith to God's free gift of salvation by putting their trust in Christ. It only takes a few moments to put your faith in Christ. It's a transaction, an event — a moment where your name is written in the Book of Life (Revelation 20:15), you are sealed with the Holy Spirit (Ephesians 1:13), and you are born again (John 3:3). Evangelistic efforts are widely applauded. I often hear stories of people who were saved on this mission trip or this conference or that revival.

During Jesus' earthly ministry and the days of the early church, the term used most frequently to designate one of Jesus' followers was "disciple," or mathetes (Greek for "learner" or "pupil"). Instead of being a one-time event like salvation, discipleship is an ongoing process, a journey through which we grow as disciples and learners of Christ. We engage personally in discipleship when we begin relationships for the purpose of helping others look more like Christ. Discipleship is not as widely applauded as evangelism, as a person usually only disciples one to three people at a time.

Furthermore, the process is not finite, but rather ongoing. It's not one big event, but more of a journey. Discipleship is also hard work. When I'm speaking at a meeting out of state and ten people decide to trust Christ, I'm encouraged and thankful to the Lord, but I return home and continue on with other aspects of my life. Someone else has the job of coming beside these young believers to help them learn, grow, say no to sin and yes to righteousness, and so on:

> "We proclaim him, admonishing and teaching everyone with all wisdom, so that we may present everyone perfect in Christ. To this end I labor, *struggling* with all his energy, which so powerfully works in me" (Colossians 1:28,29, NIV, italics mine).

Christians are exhorted not only to explain the gospel, but also to help people mature in their spirituality. The fact that Paul says he "labors and struggles" is a good eye-opener for us to understand that this is not an easy responsibility. It is doable, especially with the Holy Spirit working "powerfully" within us, but let us not have a romanticized idea that it will be easy. Although the role of disciple making is a wonderful privilege, it is one that takes time, patience, vulnerability, and often a soul-wrenching love for the disciple.

Discipleship as a Lifestyle

For some of you reading this book, discipleship is not your primary job. Maybe you work in an office and help with the church youth group twice a week. Perhaps you're a stay-at-home mom who seeks to have a ministry in your neighborhood. Maybe you're a student who wants to invest your college years in others. Each of these examples is terrific, and I am proud that you desire to learn to disciple others while living out your other responsibilities.

Others of you are in full-time vocational ministry. Perhaps you're on the staff of a local church leading the women's ministry. Or maybe you're a missionary, or are involved in some other type of full-time Christian work. I want to speak specifically to this group for a minute, as I relate especially to this. My encouragement is not to let discipleship or evangelism become just your job. You'll need to make an extra effort for it to be your lifestyle.

For example, it could be easy for us to stop our business of ministering to others when we leave work. I understand this mentality because I feel this temptation at times. We spend so much energy initiating conversations, preparing for discipleship appointments, etc, that going home and continuing to do that in our free time can feel tiring. However, telling others about Christ and walking alongside them as they grow in their relationship with God needs to be who we are, not what we do. It needs to be an overflow from our heart, not another duty to which we attend when "on the clock."

One way I look for opportunities to share my faith and disciple others "off the clock" is to put myself in situations where I can be salt and light to others. I purposefully enter into arenas where there might not be very many believers. One example is at the gym where I take group fitness classes. I figure if I'm going to spend so many hours a week working on my health, I want to have it count for eternity as well. Each time I go to the gym, I try to remember names of people I've met so I can greet them. I start up conversations by reading people's T-shirts and inquiring about them. I smile, say "Good morning," hold the door open, etc. This way, I minister through who I am instead of what I do.

I look for opportunities to pray for people. A woman in my aerobics class mentioned that her mom was very ill. I prayed for her mom on my own and then asked how she was doing the next time I saw my friend. Another woman told me she wouldn't be at the gym for a while because she was going to have a hysterectomy. I asked to pray with her to have a safe surgery and a speedy recovery. She agreed, and we prayed together in the group fitness room. An employee of the gym approached me one day and asked if I could recommend a good church because, as she put it, "It's time for me to get on track."

This same process can be applied to a scrapbooking group, dance lessons, a community college course, bowling group, children's play group, etc. If there is a coffee shop you frequent, get to know the employees and learn their names. A few years ago I got to know Sherlyn, the young girl who always fixed my hot chocolate at a nearby coffee shop. I made a habit of greeting her and making small talk with her. Over time we became friends. One morning I asked if she'd like to come to church with me. She not only came, but also rededicated her life to Christ. Later, she ended up meeting her husband at my church, and now they're both full-time missionaries!

Let me be the first to tell you that this is not tiring or draining. In fact, it's just the opposite! To share my faith and help people mature in their relationship with God "off the clock" gives me energy, enthusiasm, and excitement. To see the Lord working at my gym or coffee shop and using me as His vessel in the process is a thrill. So guard against making discipleship and evangelism a job — let it be your lifestyle.

What Is Unique About Women Discipling Women?

This is a difficult question to answer, since it's all I've ever known. This has been my life's work, and consequently it's a challenge for me to talk about what is unique about it. I've always had a woman discipler and only disciple women myself. However, a few things do come to mind.

First, women don't need to go out and play a sport together to feel a bond. We can feel bonded simply by sitting in a coffee shop and crying at some point in our time together. Second, the unique struggles we face — the sheer amount of time we give to food, caring for children, self-esteem, and hormone swings — all play into women's discipleship relationships. Third, we are more verbal in our makeup, and thus will talk a good deal about what we are learning, experiencing, and feeling. Talking and self-disclosure are non-negotiable.

Helpful Terms

The terms listed below will be used throughout the book. I've defined each one to help you better understand my intentions as you read.

Disciple — the learner in the relationship or the woman being discipled. This woman is responsible for taking the things she learns and investing them into another at some point down the line. As Chris Adsit says in his excellent book Personal Disciplemaking, "A disciple is a person in process who is eager to learn and apply the truths that Jesus Christ teaches him, which will result in ever-deepening commitments to a Christ-like lifestyle."

Discipler — the teacher, or the woman who is discipling another woman. As the leader in the relationship, she is responsible for loving, encouraging, and patiently walking alongside the disciple in her spiritual walk.

Discipleship Appointment — a regular time at which the disciple and discipler meet. This could perhaps be a weekly or bi-weekly appointment in a one-on-one or small-group setting. The time frame, depending on schedules, could be an hour or two and is spent in prayer, teaching, and training the disciple in basic skills such as faith sharing and discipling. This time is also used to study the Bible, hold each other accountable, and do outreach together.

Discipleship Chain — the term used to describe a scenario in which a woman is discipling a woman who in turn is discipling another woman. We see this example in 2 Timothy 2:2: "And the things you have heard me say in the presence of many witness, entrust to reliable men who will also be qualified to teach others" (NIV). To illustrate:

Paul > Timothy > reliable men > others

This would be a four-deep discipleship chain. One of the primary goals in discipleship is that the woman in whom you're investing your life will turn around and invest in the life of at least one other woman as well.

Why Not?

I think there are a variety of reasons that women don't engage in the discipleship endeavor. These include:

❋ Lack of knowledge

❋ Absence of a positive discipleship model

❋ Time crunch

❋ Feelings of inadequacy

❋ Lack of eternal perspective

❋ A church without a structure for discipleship relationships

My hope is that through the pages of this book, I'll be able to dismantle some of these seeming roadblocks and give you the encouragement to embrace anew the privilege of discipleship.

In Summary

Making disciples is not simply a good idea; it is a biblical mandate with which we as believers have been entrusted. We need to share our faith and make disciples of the next generation of believers. We have the help of the Holy Spirit working powerfully within us and other fellow believers beside us. Ensuring that evangelism and discipleship are not just a job (if you're in full-time vocational ministry) will ensure that ministry is an overflow of your life, not just a task to accomplish from 9 to 5 (or 9 to 9 for some of us!). Through the course of this book, we will learn to remove roadblocks to discipleship and be encouraged to begin walking alongside one another in discipleship right now!

 CHAPTER 2

The Discipler and Her Relationship with God

"When is this going to be over?" I thought to myself. I'd been meeting with Stephanie for almost an hour. I kept secretly glancing at my watch, waiting for the minutes to tick by.

It wasn't that she was boring or that I was tired; I was simply a bit off that day. I didn't have much to offer. I felt spiritually dry. Carrying the weight of unanswered prayers, unconfessed sin, and a burdensome schedule that had squeezed God out had led to this empty, spiritual hole in which I found myself. Yet life goes on, and today was the day I normally met Stephanie at a Chili's restaurant for our regular discipleship time. So here we were. I was her "spiritual" leader — and yet I felt she could probably teach me more that day than I could teach her.

For various reasons, there will be times when we feel far from God or are not as in tune with His voice and leading as we would like. Over the years I have noticed that when I feel this way, it affects my discipleship relationships as well. Feeling as if I have nothing to offer and few (if any) encouraging words is a direct result of feeling distant and discouraged in my own relationship with the Lord. Below are a few suggestions I've learned over time that may help you put your focus back on the Lord when you feel it has drifted.

Growing with God

Time with Him

Spending regular one-on-one time with the Lord is the primary way we can grow closer to Him. Just as spending time with a new friend or significant other will enable the relationship to grow deeper and more special, spending regular time with God will allow your spiritual relationship to deepen and mature.

Through the years, I've spent this time alone with God in various ways. There are many ways to spend time with God, but always be sure to include time for reading and meditating on His Word, and communicating with Him. Currently, I begin my time with God by reading the One Year Bible. As I read the different passages, I desire to learn new things about God. I also spend time looking for ways to apply what I am reading to my own life. I might read a verse that encourages me, strengthens me, or corrects an area of my life or behavior. I then spend time writing to the Lord in my journal (I have tons of these journals, all stashed in boxes under my bed). I write to Him about my feelings, things in my life for which I am thankful, and words of surrender to His plans for the day. I sometimes sing worship songs, get on my knees to pray, or memorize a verse.

Protect the Time

Whether you are a full-time vocational minister, volunteer with your church's youth group, or a witness to people in your office, you lead a busy life. Discipling people can be demanding and draining at times. There will always be the temptation to squeeze out your time with God to get other urgent things accomplished. Be careful not to allow business to crowd out your regular time with Jesus.

Often when I sit down to spend time with God, I feel tempted to start working. The battle begins in my head with thoughts such as, "I think I'll go ahead and check my email," or, "I need to organize my desk before I read my Bible," or perhaps, "I'll pay my bills so I won't forget later." The battle goes on and on. Can you relate?

There are a number of ways I've learned through the years to combat those thoughts. One is to think of Scriptures such as Matthew 6:33: "*Seek first* his kingdom and his righteousness and all these things will be given to you as well" (NIV, italics mine). Another is to say to myself, "Lori, once you start working, it will be ten times harder to stop and spend time with God." Or I will go to another room so the cluttered desk or unmade bed or whatever is screaming to be done at that moment is not catching my eye. Mostly, though, I am able to keep my regular time with Jesus when I think about how I don't want to go one day without Him. I need Him and love Him and want to be close to Him. I encourage you to remember, as busy as life gets, not to neglect that personal, devotional time with God.

Fasting

Another discipline that has been very helpful through the years in my relationship with God is fasting. In different seasons of life I've fasted in different ways. For numerous years I would fast one day a week for my dad to be saved, or for a particular struggle to be broken off in my life, or for a friend to turn back to Jesus.

I have also fasted with others. I remember a time when Nikki (a girl I discipled years ago) and I fasted together for three days. We got together each day to pray for each other and share what we were learning in the process. It was a wonderful time of seeking God and growing in our relationship as friends.

Fasting is a great opportunity to deepen your relationship with God as you depend on Him for sustenance while you're not eating. I have found the benefits of fasting far outweigh the momentary feelings of hunger. For example, when I am tempted to sin and break fellowship with God, I tell myself, "Lori, God gave you the strength to say no to food during your fast, and He has given you the strength to say no to this as well." Also, there is a refining agent when depending on God to get you through a day (or longer) of not eating that strips you of anything you might have been putting before Him. For guidelines and information on fasting, please see www.lorijoiner.com.

Scripture Memorization

I also enjoy memorizing Scripture as a way to develop and deepen my relationship with God. I am very encouraged when I memorize verses that speak of God's love, His plans for me, and His sovereignty. Some of my favorites are:

> "The Lord is righteous in all his ways and loving toward all he has made" (Psalm 145:17, NIV).

"My soul yearns for you in the night; in the morning my spirit longs for you" (Isaiah 26:9, NIV).

"The Lord will work out his plans for my life — for your faithful love, O Lord, endures forever" (Psalm 138:8, NLT).

"The moment you began praying, a command was given. I am here to tell you what it was, for God loves you very much" (Daniel 9:23, NLT).

"'For my thoughts are not your thoughts, neither are your ways my ways,' declares the Lord. 'As the heavens are higher than the earth, so are my ways higher than your ways and my thoughts than your thoughts'" (Isaiah 55:8,9, NIV).

These are just a few of the many spiritual disciplines and ideas for strengthening your walk with God and falling deeper in love with Him. The bottom line is to spend time with God and continually grow in your relationship with Him. Unfortunately, you'll find that it can be easy to neglect your relationship with Him in the midst of ministering to others, but He should be your number one priority.

Common Pitfalls

There are many pitfalls that will hinder our relationship with God and ultimately hinder our discipleship relationships as well. I have included a few pitfalls I can fall into and some helpful ideas to help you steer clear.

Living Off Yesterday

One common pitfall in our relationship with God is "living off of yesterday" — that is, yesterday's quiet times, yesterday's stories of witnessing, etc. We need a vital, growing walk with God that remains current. If you find yourself using the same example month after month, year after year, it is time to develop some new ones. Look for new opportunities to share your faith, pray with others, and discover new nuggets of wisdom in the Word. He has already put people in your life to talk to and share with, so ask Him for the eyes to see and the faith to begin conversations about Him. When you spend time with Him, ask the Holy Spirit to illuminate His Word and show you new ways to apply scripture to your life. You don't need to try to manufacture this in your own strength; God will guide you. He wants you to have a vital, growing walk with Him more than you do! Be careful not to live off of yesterday.

Not Being Real

Another pitfall is not being authentic with disciples about your relationship with God. For example, one morning I snoozed the alarm clock so many times that by the time I got up, I barely had time to shower and run to my early-morning meeting. I prayed in the shower, as I knew that probably would be the only time I would have one-on-one time with Jesus that day. In the afternoon, I hung out with one of my disciples named Brandi. I told her about hitting "snooze" on my alarm clock (it's a four-minute snooze, meaning I hit the button every four minutes for an entire hour!). I wanted her to know that I'm not perfect. I also wanted her to know I wasn't walking around under a cloud of condemnation for not having spent time reading my Bible that day.

Most people have a phantom in their head of what they "should" be doing, or compare themselves by saying, "I'll never measure up to (fill in the name)'s relationship with God." We should not act like something we're not. Transparency is the key to helping your disciples see you're not perfect and might not have your quiet time every single day.

I remember listening to a preacher say that in 30 years he had never missed one day in spending time with God. Talk about a heavy burden. I immediately thought, I could never live up to that. I could not even relate to that. I think I would have connected with him so much better if he had mentioned that he occasionally "snoozed" his clock every four minutes for an hour and got up late. I'm simply trying to make the point that when you do miss time with God, or eat when you planned to fast, or get frustrated in traffic, share that with the women you are discipling so they can relate to you. This will help them walk in grace and not feel like they have to live up to or measure up to an unattainable standard.

Hidden Sin

Nothing can hinder a relationship with God like hidden sin. This is the type of sin for which we need help from others to overcome, and yet we continue to keep it to ourselves. It's hard to minister to women when there is hidden sin in your life. Hidden sin becomes such a cycle that it can hinder your relationships with women and with God.

For example, let's say you are hiding the fact that you are going too far physically with your boyfriend. You want to spend time with God, but you feel guilty for your sins. Though you ask for forgiveness, you're aware you'll probably mess up in this area again, so your repentance is only half-hearted. When you spend time with your disciple, you don't really feel God can use you, so you stay on the surface during your time with her without diving into deeper conversation. You feel as if it would probably be a good idea to get some accountability with another Christian sister, but you write that off, thinking she will be judgmental toward you. Furthermore, you're also engaged in a spiritual battle with Satan, who is whispering lies in your direction to the effect of "God can't use you" or "You shouldn't be discipling people with this sin in your life," or even "You can't ask anyone for help because they won't look up to you anymore." Does this sound familiar?

Whatever the sin, ask God with whom you should share it, and then obey Him completely and wholeheartedly. Having a right, tender relationship with God is worth the temporary embarrassment you might feel. Being able to minister with a clear conscience to the women God has placed in your life is worth it as well. Don't let hidden sin hinder you from touching the lives of women and storing up treasure in heaven.

Forgetting We Are in a Battle

Everyone is engaged in a spiritual battle, and whether we want to be or not is irrelevant. If you try to walk with God in any capacity, the devil will try to stop you by whatever means possible. Additionally, if you are sharing your faith and discipling others, you are an even greater threat to Satan. He'll work overtime to get you off track, discouraged, and isolated. Warren Wiersbe, a Bible scholar, has said, "Sooner or later every believer discovers that the Christian life is a battleground, not a playground, and that he faces an enemy who is much stronger than he is apart from the Lord."

Our struggle is not against flesh and blood. It is not against what we can see. Satan and his demons are not a fantasy; they are very real. If we desire to obey God and resist the devil, we are in for a struggle. Some biblical descriptions of Satan are:

"I saw Satan fall like lightning from Heaven" (Luke 10:18, NIV).

"The thief comes only to steal, kill and destroy …" (John 10:10, NIV).

"Your enemy the devil prowls around like a roaring lion looking for someone to devour" (1 Peter 5:8, NIV).

"The God of this age has blinded the minds of unbelievers so they cannot see the light of the gospel …" (2 Corinthians 4:4, NIV).

"We know that we are children of God and that the whole world is under the control of the evil one" (1 John 5:19, NIV).

"Finally, be strong in the Lord and in his mighty power. Put on the full armor of God so that you can take your stand against the devil's schemes. For our struggle is not against flesh and blood, but against the rulers, against the authorities, against the powers of this dark world and against the spiritual forces of evil in the heavenly realms" (Ephesians 6:10-12, NIV).

We're in a battle. I know some days it doesn't feel that way, but be aware that Satan is scheming against you. He and his demons will do everything possible to keep you from fulfilling the purpose and plan God has for you. Just as God desires to spend time with you, so Satan desires to keep you from your appointment with God at all costs. Be ever mindful that you are in a spiritual battle, and that battle can hinder your discipleship relationships.

In Summary

Maintaining a vital, close walk with the Lord needs to be the top priority in your life, whether you are discipling a woman or not. However,
it is all the more important if you are discipling a woman. Spending
time with Him on a consistent basis, and engaging in spiritual disciplines such as fasting and Scripture memory, can help deepen your love
relationship with God. A good understanding of common pitfalls in our
relationship with God, such as living off yesterday, not being authentic,
and hidden sin in our lives, will help us guard against these things in our
own lives. God wants our heart to be steadfast in love with Him. After
all, it's not our good works and tons of disciples He is ultimately after —
it's our heart.

 **CHAPTER 3**

S.T.A.R.T. Discipling

While there are probably dozens of attributes one can look for in a woman to potentially disciple, five of the foundational characteristics to identify are: Spirit-filled, teachable, available, reliable, and able to transfer what she learns. We have a limited amount of time each day to dedicate to discipling women. Because of this limited time factor, we need to be careful in our discipleship choices. A helpful acronym to remember when deciding who to disciple is S.T.A.R.T. — knowing what to look for before you begin discipling someone.

Spirit-Filled

When you desire to begin discipling, it is important for you to look for a woman who is Spirit-filled, meaning she asks God to be in control of her life and direct her path step by step each day. This is a woman who wants to follow Christ and seeks to learn and grow in her relationship with Him. She displays a life surrendered to the Lordship of Christ.

She is willing to follow the voice and promptings of God when it is easy as well as when it goes against her own will.

Look for clues to this in her life. Does she pray? Has she mentioned something in her life she is struggling with and for which she is seeking God's help and direction? Has she mentioned an example in her life where she felt God was prompting her to do something that took a step of faith, and did she follow through?

Discipling a woman who is not Spirit-filled will feel like a dead end. If she does not want to follow God wholeheartedly and follow His leading in different situations, or if she senses God is wanting her to take a step of faith and she flatly refuses, you will begin to wonder why you are discipling her. The reason we disciple women is to help them look more like Christ and be able to disciple others in the future. Not being Spirit-filled blocks both goals.

Teachable

Discipling women who are teachable is another key characteristic to look for when deciding whom to disciple. You want to disciple women who are willing to be taught new things, and who are open to correction and wise counsel. If she does not have this character trait, you're going to have a tough time teaching her anything new, especially if it means some type of necessary change in her life.

To many women, discipleship sounds fun at first. It's a blessing to have another woman care about you, spend time with you, and teach you things from the Bible. But when you come across a passage that signals a need for change in her life and she is consistently resistant, it will be tough. If you notice a personality trait that needs attention, and she responds by saying, "That's just how I am" and refuses to change, you're going to have a difficult time helping this disciple mature spiritually.

A good example of teachability involves Alyssa. She not only wanted to be discipled, she was ready to make any changes needed to grow in her walk with God. One afternoon I talked with her about her relationship with her parents and her need to take more ownership of her finances.

"Alyssa," I said, "I think it's time you have your own checking account and insurance, and pay your own phone bill. You're a graduate student and are always complaining about your parents being controlling. If they continue to pay your bills, they'll continue to have control."

"It's hard, Lori," Alyssa replied. "I don't know how to talk to them in a way that they'll listen."

I responded by saying, "You need to let them know that you are thankful for all the ways they have helped you financially, but in order to become the adult you need to be, it is time you took responsibility for these areas of your life."

Instead of saying, "Lori, these are my parents and I'll deal with it," Alyssa was grateful and respected my advice. I was not trying to run her life; I simply saw that this issue was holding her back from becoming an adult and taking responsibility in life.

In contrast, on a mission trip one summer, I was assigned to live and work with Jenny. She was a pretty girl with a slim figure and beautiful brown hair. She was also very quiet and often isolated herself. Halfway though the summer, I had a conversation with her regarding her choice of clothing, explaining that some of the clothes she wore were rather revealing and distracting. Although she said she would dress more modestly, I never saw any change. I also brought up suspicions that she was throwing up her food. She flatly denied it, but continued to excuse herself from the table after dinner to purge.

Jenny was not teachable. I am really not sure why she came on the mission trip; she seemed uninterested in learning or being challenged, or perhaps she was simply reluctant to change her lifestyle. You can imagine the frustration I felt that summer, as well as the distraction she was to the girls with her eating habits and to the guys with her dress.

Teachability is essential in a potential disciple. One of the very basic elements of discipleship is that you are teaching her how to walk with God and grow in her relationship with Him. So keep this in mind as you pray for women to disciple.

Available

Another attribute to look for in a potential disciple is availability. In other words, does she have time to get together for discipleship, to spend time together, and to be a part of a church in come capacity?

"I want to get involved in this organization and would love to be discipled," Anna said with much enthusiasm. Anna and I were sitting outside at a big picnic. She had her hair pulled up in a ponytail and had come up and introduced herself earlier. "Well, Anna, tell me about yourself — do you work?" I asked. "Do you have any hobbies?"

"Oh, yes," Anna answered. "I am in a sorority and a business fraternity, I volunteer three days a week at an inner-city youth program, and I am also training for a marathon." This was all on top of her regular college class load and a part-time job. Just listening to her made me tired. She seemed unavailable; every minute of her day was booked. I was unsure where she thought she had the time to dedicate to discipleship and where she would have time to eventually disciple another. My response to her, after hearing about all her activities, went something like this:

"Anna, I'd love for you to get involved and eventually be discipled, but there are a few things you will need to consider before we start. First, discipleship is a commitment that involves time. As you explain what you have going on, I am concerned that there is not time for you to get together with a woman to be discipled, to hang out as friends, or for you to eventually pass on to another woman what you have learned. I think all the things you are doing are great. Perhaps, though, you may need to curb some of your many activities to make time for this new relationship in your life."

Anna did curb some of her activities and suspended others for a season as well. She went on to not only be discipled, but also to disciple, touching many women's lives for God's glory!

The bottom line is that if the woman is unavailable, busy, and completely over-committed, you'll find it difficult to spend regular time together. Furthermore, she won't have time eventually to disciple another.

Reliable

Reliability is a key characteristic to look for in women you want to potentially disciple. If I am leading a small group of women at my home, for example, and I think I would like to disciple one of the ladies, I am going to consider her reliability. Does she follow through on things she is delegated to do? Does she keep her word, upholding commitments even if something seemingly more fun arises? I asked a friend of mine,

Alicia, if she could recall an example of a prospective disciple who was unreliable. She immediately said yes.

"I tried to disciple a girl a number of years ago. She was precious and we could talk for hours," Alicia said. "The only problem was that she was not reliable. I would give her a small assignment for the next week, like read the first chapter of the Gospel of John so we could discuss it the next time we get together, and the young woman would show up to our time together and would not have read it. This was a problem because I had planned and prepared for us to learn and talk about that chapter, and she had not done what I asked. I would always make the best of it, but it would happen again and again. She never really progressed; we couldn't move forward because she would not do anything outside of our time together that I thought was necessary for her continued growth in the Lord."

One thing we need to make sure as to do as disciplers is to be clear in what we are asking of the women with which we are meeting. We can't fault them for being unreliable if we frequently change plans on them, don't give clear information, or are vague about what we are asking.

Transferable

I cannot stress this point enough. The ability to transfer what we learn to another woman is paramount. The reason we disciple is for the woman to look more like Christ each day and for her to pass onto others what she has learned. I talked about this at length in chapter 1, "A Biblical Perspective on Discipleship." This may be a bit harder to spot, as you might not have seen her in this role. But you can look for character traits, like being others-focused and willing to help other women. Perhaps she has shared a burden for a woman she knows who needs help.

When these characteristics are evident, it signals to me that they are willing to be involved in other women's lives and, with a bit of guidance, will be able to transfer things they learn.

The woman you are meeting with, or want to begin meeting with, needs to know that transference of what she has learned to another is part of discipleship. From the very first time I meet with a woman to do follow-up if she is a new believer, or in doing a commitment sheet (see Chapter 7, "Commitment to Discipleship") I am saying things like, "I want to teach you this thoroughly so you can, one day, share it with another." I sat down with three women I discipled from my church and said, "My hope for each of you is that you get the thrill and joy of discipling another group of women like I have with each of you!" So right from the beginning, clearly explain that transferability is an integral part of the discipleship relationship.

Second, the woman needs to emotionally be up for transferring what she knows to another. Whether you are discipling a woman sitting next to you in your office, or your neighbor, or (for me) a woman at my gym, I am making sure they not only know the expectation but also that they are up for it in their heart. It is okay for her to be nervous. She may say something like, "I wouldn't know what to do!" You can reply, "That's okay; I can help you. You will basically be doing with her what I am going to do with you. I will walk you through it!"

Nikkea is a woman I discipled for years. She is an African-American beauty and has a heart to transfer what she knows to other women so they can pass it along to other women and so on. It was my joy to watch Nikkea gain confidence in sharing her faith, taking new believers through follow-up lessons, and eventually disciple countless women. She is having and has had an amazing impact on other women as she takes them under her wing, helps and disciples them in the faith, and challenges them to disciple another as she has done them! At one point we were able to count a discipleship chain five-deep!

The Great Exception: New Believers

"Hi, Allison," I said as I walked into Gold's Gym. I noticed that she seemed especially downcast and sad that day.

"Oh, hi, Lori," she answered.

"Are you alright? I have never seen you looking so down."

I had gotten to know Allison over the past month. Often, when I came in to work out, she was behind the front desk greeting people. I knew she was not a Christian and was intentionally building a relationship with her.

"Things aren't going well at home, and I'm in a lot of pain," she said as she glanced down at her very pregnant stomach. "My back is really hurting today, and I can hardly stand here."

"Allison, I'll be praying for you today," I told her. "I'm so sorry things aren't going well." After we talked for a while, I continued in this manner: "I'm not sure what you think about spiritual things, but I'd love to invite you to my church. I think you'd be very encouraged there."

"I'd love to go," Allison said, "but I won't understand anything. I mean, I won't know what they're talking about."

"Well, how about you and I get together this week, and I'll share with you about God and some of the basic teachings of the Bible, and explain what church will be like."

"Oh, that'd be great," Allison said.

When we met up, I shared the simple gospel message with her, and she readily put her trust in Christ. She came to church with me that Sunday and took Communion as a new believer. Praise God!

When you lead a woman to Christ, you need to begin meeting with her immediately. Don't wait to see if she is Spirit-filled, teachable, available, reliable and has the ability to transfer what she learns. You need to get involved in her life and begin to meet with her for at least four weeks to do basic follow-up (four basic lessons for every new believer). When a woman puts her faith in Christ, the Holy Spirit, who comes to live in her heart, will lead her to hunger more for God and grow in her relationship with Him. Therefore, begin to disciple her immediately. I would also recommend, as I did with Allison, bringing her to church, a home-based small group, and anything else she might be able to fit into her schedule.

How to Begin

If you have observed a woman to be Spirit-filled, teachable, available, reliable and able to transfer what she learns, I suggest you go out to eat, grab coffee, or otherwise spend time together. Explain that you see these qualities in her and would like to start a discipleship relationship. Be specific in this area, encouraging her with what you have observed.

For example, instead of saying, "You're really teachable," say instead, "The other day when we talked about how to organize the singles' Valentine's

Day party, you were really observant, you wrote things down, and asked good questions. I appreciate your heart to learn and for being so teachable." Or instead of saying, "You're reliable," say, "Jackie, I've noticed that you have great priorities and can be depended upon for important tasks. Your reliability is a terrific asset and a great example to others."

After you have encouraged her and told her the great things you've observed about her, extend an invitation to her and give her the opportunity to think about it and respond: "I'd love to get to know you better and possibly develop a discipleship relationship with you. Why don't we spend today just getting to know each other better, and next week I'll bring some materials, a short Bible study and a sheet that will outline this relationship." For more explanation on these materials, see Chapter 7, "Commitment to Discipleship."

In Summary

We have a limited amount of time each day to dedicate to discipling other people. A helpful acronym to apply evaluating potential disciples is S.T.A.R.T. Look for women who are Spirit-filled, Teachable, Available, and Reliable women, with the ability to Transfer what they learn. Be careful not to commit to discipling just anyone who asks, or the woman who seems neediest in your Bible study or Sunday school class. Stop, wait, and observe her carefully. If one of the above traits is missing, you will be frustrated in your discipleship endeavors. Also, keep in mind that if you lead a woman to faith in Christ, you need to immediately begin to meet with her for follow-up and help her get started in her new relationship with Christ regardless of where she is within the above acronym.

 CHAPTER 4

The Appointment

"Lord, I'm kinda busy here…"

I sat in the local laundry working on some projects I had brought to pass the time. As I sat there, though, I felt the gentle nudge of the Lord prompting me to strike up a conversation with the older African-American woman sitting across from me. "Lord, I would talk to her if I did not have so many other things to do," I argued. "Besides, what in the world would I have in common with her to talk about?"

The next time I glanced up at her, she was holding a gospel booklet she had found laying on top of the washing machine. "Okay, Lord, I get the hint," I acknowledged. "Here we go."

"Hi, my name is Lori . . . I noticed you were reading a booklet about God? I have a relationship with God and would love to talk to you about it further if you have any questions." (Yes, it was about that awkward and abrupt.)

"My name is Belinda," she answered. "I've been thinking I need to go to church."

What transpired from there was the beginning of a new life in Christ for Belinda and a wonderful friendship and discipleship relationship between us. After Belinda put her trust in Jesus as her Lord and Savior that day, I began explaining to her the need for us to meet regularly to talk, pray, and study the Bible together. "Belinda," I said, "just like a small child learns how to crawl, and then walk, and then run, you are a young babe in Christ, and it is important for you to grow and mature in your relationship with Christ, and I would love to help you in that process."

To walk alongside another woman in discipleship is such a fulfilling endeavor. My discipleship relationship with Belinda looked different than the one with a friend from church who was my age and single, and that relationship looked different the one with a college woman I was discipling. You see, to some degree, discipleship is a reflection of each woman's individual personality. And even though it will look different from woman to woman, when it comes to the discipleship appointment, there is a set of essential elements, a framework, to help you cover a variety of areas in your disciples' growth process. Those essential elements are small talk, accountability, content, prayer, and outreach. So, whether you've been discipling a woman for a long time or just beginning, a thorough study of each element will give a helpful framework in which to plan the discipleship time together.

Five Essential Elements

Small Talk

This involves getting to know your disciple and the different areas of her life. In small talk, you want to find out about her family and children, significant other, hobbies, job details, etc. It's important to care about all aspects of a person's life, not just the spiritual side. Don't forget to share about your own life as well.

Accountability

Accountability comes when we reveal the real struggles and short-comings in our lives in order to receive help, guidance, and support. It requires vulnerability and authenticity. In accountability, both women share current struggles and agree to ask each other about those struggles regularly, pray, and encourage each other toward complete victory. I usually present my struggles first because I have found that it helps the woman I am meeting with feel more comfortable to talk about her own.

Content

A discipleship appointment does not merely consist of meeting together to talk and catch up. It needs substance. There is content involved, since you are discipling this woman with an end in mind. Your ultimate goal is to help her to grow as a mature believer and to become like Christ. You are also developing her to be able to disciple another woman in the future. The content portion of an appointment involves teaching her something new. This segment could consist of time studying the Word, learning a practical skill such as how to tell others about her faith in Christ, or perhaps reading a book or workbook together on a particular subject. For some ideas as far as what content to use, see Chapter 10, "Materials for Growth."

Prayer

I hardly ever begin or end a discipleship appointment without prayer. It is the Lord who is the master discipler, and I am merely a tool in His hand. So I regularly, through prayer, invite the Lord to take His rightful place in the discipleship time together as the Author and Perfecter of our faith. You can also use this time to teach and model to your disciple how to pray. For example, she may be nervous about praying out loud, confused about what types of things she can pray for, or even at a loss concerning how to address the Lord. Spend time praying that God would help both of you apply what was learned that day, for things shared during accountability or small talk, and for the outreach part of the appointment. I also leave some time to pray for spiritually lost people in our lives, whether family members, friends, acquaintances, or strangers.

Outreach

Reaching out to others will be best passed on from you to your disciple if you model this well. I have found it fairly easy to include this element into my discipleship time if I have planned ahead. For example, if discipling a woman from church, perhaps you could spend the last part of your appointment visiting a newcomer to your Sunday school class or home-based fellowship group. If you're in ministry outside the local church, spend time with a visitor who recently attended a weekly meeting or Bible study. If the disciple is part of your youth ministry, take her to visit someone she has gotten to know at school, or a student who has attended your weekly youth group meeting. A great way to reach out to a mother is by volunteering to help with her kids. This shows real care for the mom. And besides being a huge blessing to her, it might open the door for future conversations about Christ.

During the outreach part of the appointment, spend time getting to know the woman by asking general questions about her life, interests, and hobbies. You might transition into a more spiritual conversation by asking, "Did you grow up going to church?" or "Was the other morning your first time at church?" Follow up by asking, "Were you able to understand everything that was talked about, or was some of it confusing?" The bottom line is to find out where the woman is on her spiritual journey, and to see if you and your disciple can somehow help her towards Christ.

Getting Started

Where to Meet

You can meet your disciple almost anywhere. However, you should keep a few things in mind when deciding on a place to meet. First, you want to be somewhere devoid of distractions. I have found that coffee shops are fine, as long as the music is not blaring and I can find a table out of the flow of traffic. In my little corner of the world there are two coffee shops: Common Grounds and Coffee Haus. Common Grounds is the hip place, with great coffee and hot chocolates. Problem is, the music is sometimes so loud that I leave with a headache. I've therefore had to retreat to the Coffee Haus, which used to be an Exxon gas station. And the hot chocolates are unimpressive (is it actually possible to burn hot chocolate?). But it is quiet, and the crowd is much smaller. You will also need to find a place you enjoy and find little distraction. When getting together with a woman from work, you could meet with her at the office during pre-business hours or in an unused boardroom during lunch. Perhaps you can meet with a neighbor in your living room while your children nap.

When to Meet

Find a regular time that fits both schedules. Nanette, a teacher at a nearby elementary school, and I used to meet every Tuesday night at Souper Salad for dinner after we both got off work. By the time we had finished eating, the restaurant had pretty much cleared out, allowing us to talk without too many distractions (I might add that if you employ a table for an extended period of time, be sure to leave a generous tip for your waiter). I do not typically have standing discipleship appointments on weekends. I find that with travel, family birthday parties, etc., I'm simply not able to keep a regular appointment. For some people, though, this might be the best time of the week to meet.

How Much Time to Allot

Your appointment can take anywhere from one and a half to two hours. Much of this depends on any outreach you might have planned and the material you will cover. A sample timeline for a one-and-a-half-hour appointment could look like this:

1. Small talk (10 minutes)

2. Accountability (10 minutes)

3. Content (25 minutes)

4. Prayer (10 minutes)

5. Outreach (40 minutes)

If you are just getting started, try to plan for an hour to an hour and a half. Don't feel pressured to make the appointment long just to take up time. If you're finished, then go ahead and end it. Also, if you happen to be discipling a woman who simply is not talkative, the discipleship time might not take a full hour.

What to Bring

The Bible is always important to bring to the discipleship appointment. Another key tool is what I call a discipleship binder. In mine, I've stuck tabs listing the names of each woman I am currently meeting with. I use it at the beginning of each week to plan and record what I will do in my discipleship times throughout the week. I start with a review of past meetings and then plan for the next week. I review notes I made to myself, such as reminders to bring articles, email a weblink, or call her on her birthday.

Okay, so it would seem I'd be able to remember, week to week, the discipleship details of each woman I disciple. However, I've found it is impossible for me to remember everything I've done with them and what topics we've covered together without a good written history. This record keeping has been especially beneficial in my long-term discipleship relationships.

So go ahead and start your discipleship binder today. Write down the name of the woman you are discipling and record everything you recall from your appointments together. Include things such as Bible study lessons and practical skills you've covered. Make a note of your next appointment, the meeting place and time, and items to cover in future sessions. It's also helpful to keep a record of any significant data such as birthdays, hobbies, and goals. If she's a mother, write down the names and ages of her children, her job, and husband's name. If she's a college-aged woman, record her major, boyfriend's name, and hometown. If she's a youth, record her parents' names, home phone number, and year in school. Feel free to record any pertinent information you find helpful to connect more effectively with your disciple.

Putting the Pieces Together: The Appointment

In this section, I will walk you though a typical discipleship time so you could see firsthand how each element of a discipleship appointment flows naturally into the other. So here is a play-by-play outline of what a typical discipleship get together looks like for me:

Small Talk

"Hi, Karen," I exclaimed as she walked toward my little table in the corner. Karen is a woman I met at my church. We began meeting together each week for dinner. I enjoy our meetings because she thinks my jokes are actually funny, and I love a good audience. Although she is beautiful, with long blonde hair and a big smile, she struggles with low self-esteem and bulimia. We sat in a booth at Jason's Deli and caught each other up on our lives. I asked about her job and her family; she asked about my recent trip to see my dad and my latest home decorating project. We enjoyed the conversation and settled comfortably into the hour-and-a-half time together.

Accountability

Our conversation became more serious as we began to move past the surface news of our lives into personal hardships and struggles. I transitioned from small talk to accountability by sharing about a recent situation in which I had lied to a good friend. I explained the story about re-gifting a past Christmas gift from him, and then lying to cover it up. I told her about calling him, confessing my sin, and asking for forgiveness. I teared up as I told Karen the story; my heart was still tender to the fact that I had lied in the first place. Because I was vulnerable with her, Karen talked of her ongoing eating disorder. That week had been victorious for her. She had been stressed with work and family issues, and had wanted to eat her way to comfort. She chose not to binge, and instead went with a friend to get her nails painted! I rejoiced over this victory with her and encouraged her to keep persevering to not give into the binge temptation.

Prayer

"Karen, why don't we pray before we go any further today?" I suggested at this point. "I'll start us off, and you can close for us." Sitting in our booth together, we quietly prayed for each other. I asked God to continue to give Karen strength in regard to her eating habits and her walk with Him. She prayed for me to be truthful in the small things of life. We also sought the Lord on behalf of a young girl named Amanda, who was going to join us toward the end of our time together. We prayed that God would move in her heart and that she would place her trust in

Christ soon. We also asked God to direct our time together and to be in control of every aspect of our lives.

I reached for my discipleship binder and flipped to Karen's section. This is what I had planned for that day...

Karen, January 17

* Ask about her trip home to see her grandfather

* Accountability: my re-gifting story (or whatever else is on my heart)

* Prayer: Amanda to be saved!

* Time in Word: Galatians 1:10, breaking off fear of man lesson

* Begin working on personal testimony

* Give her handout from last week (jealousy lesson to use with her disciple, Kristin)

Content

I pulled out a short Bible study I had prepared based on Galatians 1:10. This short lesson, which I affectionately call a "nugget" from the Word, looked something like this:

Read Galatians 1 and answer the following questions:

Who is Paul writing to? What seems to be the main ideas in chapter 1?

Re-read verse 10:

How would you describe the difference between trying to win the approval of men and of God?

What are some situations in your life where you tried to win the approval of men?

What can we do to continue to be God pleasers and not men pleasers?

We spent time working though the lesson and answering the questions together. We also discussed how to prepare a personal testimony so she could articulate her faith to her family and friends. For this resource, please see www.lorijoiner.com.

"Hey, you two — I'm here," Amanda said, walking up to the table. "I'm just going to get an iced tea."

"Sure thing," I said as I got up to greet her.

Karen and I wrapped things up, and I recorded a few things in my discipleship binder for next week. I made a note to make sure Karen actually said her testimony to me out loud, and to remember to pray for the promotion at work she was hoping to get.

Outreach

Amanda returned with her iced tea, and we all began to catch up on each other's lives. I inquired about her weekend and asked if she liked the guy she had gone out with. Karen asked about what she wore on the date and whether he had asked her out again. We had met Amanda when she visited one of our socials at church, and Karen and I had asked her to grab coffee after the meeting. That night she told us that she had come to our meeting because she was curious about Christianity. She said she had attended church before but was confused about God. Since then we had been meeting every week to continue to build a relationship and talk about her questions concerning God.

After we caught up for a while, I transitioned to more spiritual matters by asking if she had thought of any more questions about Jesus since we had met the week before. She said that some of her friends had been talking about what happens to people who have never heard about Christ. I told her that was an excellent question, and we began to dialogue and read God's Word together. I first turned to Isaiah 55:8-9 in the Bible: "'For my thoughts are not your thoughts, neither are your ways my ways,' declares the Lord. 'As the heavens are higher than the earth, so are my ways higher than your ways and my thoughts than your thoughts'" (NIV).

"Amanda," I said, "God's decision about what will happen to a person who dies without ever having heard about Christ is one of those things He understands but we may not fully understand, as His thoughts are so much higher than ours. While He has not given us a definite answer, I do want to share with you some other verses that we should consider in light of this question." For this full explanation, please see www.lorijoiner.com.

A Few Thoughts on Outreach

Many times when we consider discipling another woman, the first thing that comes to our mind is usually not outreach and evangelism. But to me, they go hand in hand. We disciple women we have led to Christ through evangelism. And we can model how to reach out and witness to other women to our disciple in our daily experiences and in our discipleship time together.

I have found that it can be extremely easy to spend the entire time together talking, laughing, and learning with my disciple. But though those elements are certainly important, they shouldn't consistently crowd out outreach time. And since you need to model outreach, the discipleship time is a terrific situation in which to do it.

I remember talking with James, a Jehovah's Witness, one summer. I was on a mission trip to California, and Cherie, a woman I was discipling, was with me. There were a number of times in my conversation with James that I found myself unfamiliar with certain passages he used to explain his points. In some instances I did not know the background or context for an obscure verse he was quoting. Instead of getting nervous and fearful, I merely explained to James, "I'm unfamiliar with the background of that passage. If we set up another time to talk about our differing beliefs, I can answer that more clearly." By modeling outreach, Cherie was able to see me stay calm and gentle in the midst of the heinous twisting of Scripture and the major discrepancies in James' arguments. I'm convinced that Cherie learned more in that one hour of straight evangelism than I could have taught her in three hours of merely telling her what to do.

Flexibility

I sat down with Jeni at Chili's. I could tell something was wrong the minute I saw her.

"Jeni, you look so troubled. Is everything okay?" I asked.

"John has not been telling me the truth about his dating history," Jeni answered, "and now I'm not sure I can trust him."

John and Jeni had been dating for a year and a half and were on the verge of engagement. As she began to cry, I knew that I would not be pulling out my discipleship binder. Not only would it have been cold to push through my pre-planned agenda, I also wasn't sure she would have been able to concentrate on what I had planned. She was feeling distraught and hopeless, and her world seemed to be crashing down around her.

There have definitely been times when, after having planned down to the smallest detail for a discipleship appointment, I don't pull out the binder. And that's okay. Serious relationship issues, the death of a friend or family member, and difficult work problems are just a few of the situations I've encountered during my discipleship appointments that have caused me to change my plans.

Every so often, the Holy Spirit has led me to do something entirely different than what I had planned. In the past, He's nudged me to talk deeper about an issue that came up earlier in our conversation, and other times to focus on a different passage of Scripture altogether. Rather than push through your own pre-planned agenda, make the Lord and the woman you are meeting with the priority in your discipleship time, and adjust your plans when necessary.

Consistency

That said, be careful not to make a habit of eliminating what you've planned. You will, if you haven't already, disciple a woman who seems to always have an extenuating circumstance about which she needs to talk about at length. Discipleship is about loving her and listening to her, but it's also about giving her the tools, skills, and training she needs to handle life as a mature believer. If you're not able to equip your disciple, you aren't helping her in the long run. You will need to learn how to listen without letting an issue consistently take up the entire time.

Shelly had serious ongoing family issues at home. Her parents argued, committed adultery, separated, and eventually divorced during Shelly's college years. Week after week, Shelly and I would talk about the latest situation with her parents, and the emotional difficulties this caused her. It seemed anything could upset her. I wanted to begin to talk to her about choosing joy and being filled with the Holy Spirit, and explain that her parents were responsible for their decisions — she shouldn't have to carry the weight of their marriage. But week after week, it seemed, I could never get to these lessons because we would always run out of time.

Finally, I began to be a bit more assertive. I continued to listen and be compassionate to her situation, but I began to say, "Shelly, I'd like to teach you some things today to help you in future conversations with your parents. Let's pray for them and then we can read some verses from the Bible that I think will help." She was a bit disappointed at first, since she was used to venting to me the entire time we met. After a while, however, she began to apply the simple things we were learning and grew stronger in her faith.

While you don't want to forge ahead with discipleship plans in the face of an extenuating circumstance, neither do you want to circle the same issues every week without making any helpful progress. You need to give direction so that your disciple can move ahead in her growth. The goal for your disciple is to mature in her relationship with Christ and walk in victory, independent of you and dependent on Christ.

After the Appointment

Think through some ways you can enhance and deepen your discipleship relationship outside of the appointment. I have a basket full of stationery because I like to write encouraging notes to the women in my life, either mailing them or giving them when I see them next. Email or call them during the week.

One such call was to Brandy, one of the women I've met with. I wanted to hear about her new baby and how she was adjusting to being a stay-at-home mom. When I email, I usually include an uplifting verse telling her that I am thinking about her and praying for her.

For one Valentine's Day, I put together a care package filled with all kinds of candy, random things, and a card for Tiffany. I knew Tiffany wasn't dating anyone and would not be expecting anything on this holiday, so I sent her this care package! I wanted to surprise her and give her something to open. It's so important for the women you disciple to see you go the extra mile to love them and care for them outside the discipleship appointment.

A Few Extras

Logistics

Make sure you and your disciple have a regular time and place to meet. Don't put yourself in the position where you're calling each week to figure this out. On your first appointment, pick the most convenient time and place for the both of you, and make that the plan. For example, I know that this Tuesday I am meeting with Telawna at Chili's for lunch, and on Wednesday at 3 p.m. I am meeting with Kendra at Starbucks.

Preparation

When you pull out your notes and they see that you've thought about your time together beforehand, it honors your disciple. When the women I am discipling see me pull out my blue discipleship binder, they know I've thought about them and prayed for them. I'm not being haphazard about their spiritual growth process. Careful planning blesses, encourages, and respects them.

Time

"Hey, you two! I'm just dropping by to say hi!" Tiffany and Jennifer had opened the door of their apartment to find me standing there, balancing three large cherry limeades from Sonic. "I just wanted you to know I was thinking about you both, and thought I'd bring you a little treat."

Even though I'd been discipling Jennifer and Tiffany for two years, I wanted to make sure they knew I valued them and that our relationship was not limited to just the two hours we spent together in discipleship each week. Making time to spend with the women you disciple helps the relationship grow and deepen. You might invite them over for dinner, watch a movie, or run errands together. You could drop by their house, perhaps after they have put their kids to sleep, and share a cup of hot chocolate. I've also taken numerous road trips with the women I disciple. The late-night conversations in the car still stand out to me as some of the best memories and time spent together.

Prayer

Pray for your disciples regularly. In John 17, Jesus prays for Himself, His disciples, and the others who would become believers though them. In Luke 22:31, Jesus says, "Simon, Simon, Satan has asked to sift you as wheat. But I have *prayed for you*, Simon that your faith may not fail. And when you have turned back, strengthen your brothers" (NIV, italics mine). It's obvious from these passages and others that Jesus spent much time praying for His disciples. We should follow His example when it comes to our own disciples.

In Summary

Discipleship will look a little different from woman to woman, as each discipleship relationship is unique. However, there are five basic elements that each discipleship time should include. These are small talk, accountability, prayer, content, and outreach. I don't tend to wander far from these five elements in my discipleship appointments.

There will be times when flexibility will be needed. However, be sure to maintain consistency within the discipleship time to ensure that the woman is actually developing and moving forward in her Christian maturity. Furthermore, take care not to neglect the very important component of outreach. Modeling outreach to your disciple will help her have a fruitful witness for Christ in the future. I've found prayer for my disciple, good thorough planning, and dependence on the Holy Spirit to be key in my discipleship relationships.

 **CHAPTER 5**

Beginning with Evangelism

-----**Original Message**-----

From: Gina Holly

To: Lori Joiner

Subject: Questions

Hey Lori! I hope you had a wonderful Thanksgiving. My break was pretty good, but really crazy with all the family around and all. I still definitely have questions… My first question is, am I allowed to pray if I haven't put my faith in Christ yet, cuz I totally pray all the time. My second questions is, how do I know when I'm ready to put my faith in Christ? I think I'm ready, but I don't know for sure… My last question is that why don't miracles like the splitting of the Red Sea, or crazy things like that happen anymore? I mean, I know miracles still happen, but not extreme ones, and I was just wondering why. Anyhow, I'd love your input... okay, I'm gonna let you go now! I'll see you on Tuesday.

Gina

-----**Original Message**-----
From: Lori Joiner
To: Gina Holly
Subject: RE: Questions

Hi Gina! I loved reading your email and am excited to meet with you soon. Yes, you can pray to God before you put your faith in Him. God loves you and desires to have a relationship with you and talking to Him (prayer) is a good way to communicate with God. As far as how to know you are ready, I think you are ready, Gina. You're already talking to God. It's like you have a relationship with Him already but haven't actually put your whole trust and faith in Him. You can do this alone, or with me and Allissa when we meet. It's between you and God Gina.

As far as the miracles-they do still happen today! All the time! People are healed, storms cease, etc. I can tell you some amazing stories when we get together. I am glad you had a good thanksgiving! See ya soon!

In Him, Lori

Where to Find Disciples

There are many places to find people who need someone to walk alongside them and begin to disciple them, to help them grow and

BEGINNING WITH EVANGELISM

mature spiritually. Look around you. If you are in a home fellowship group, a young marrieds class, or a women's Bible study, there are people likely trying to grow in their relationship with God who would be very encouraged to have someone intentionally helping them. In my various activities, I keep my eye out for people I can help, walk beside, and encourage.

Another way to locate possible disciples is to share your faith and begin building relationships with women before they put their faith in Christ. An example is Gina from the email exchange I just shared. When I met Gina she was spiritually searching. I invited her to have coffee with my friend Allissa and me, and we talked at length that day about our lives, backgrounds, and Jesus. Gina felt comfortable asking us all sorts of questions about God, the Bible, and how to know Christ. We continued to meet together for months afterward. In a sense, I was already discipling Gina even though she hadn't put her faith in Christ yet. I cared for her and fervently prayed for her to come to faith in Christ.

A few months later, as we were standing in line to get a cup of coffee, Gina exclaimed, "Well, Lori, today is the day!"

"For what?" I asked.

"To put my faith in Christ. I've wanted to do it all week but decided to wait and pray with you."

I want to suggest that you look around you to find women to potentially disciple. More likely than not, God has already put women in your life who are struggling in their relationship with Him. He has also planted women in your sphere of influence who need to hear the message of the gospel, put their faith in Christ, and find discipleship.

65

So Now What?

Once a woman has put her faith in Christ, you have the privilege of discipling her! As in the case with Gina, I'd already established two things in our relationship: spending time together and meeting regularly to talk about Jesus. These two things continued to happen, the only difference being that Gina was now a believer! The next time we got together we began a series of four lessons aimed at helping new believers grow in their faith:

1. How to be sure you are a Christian

2. How to experience God's love and forgiveness

3. How to understand the ministry of the Holy Spirit

4. How to mature in your relationship with Christ

For more on these lessons and how to order other helpful material, see Chapter 10, "Materials for Growth."

In Summary

Many Christians are not discipling others for a variety of reasons. One involves uncertainty regarding the disciple. I want to encourage you to look in the areas in which you're already involved — church, work, the gym — and find struggling believers or non-believers in whom you could begin to invest spiritually. I will put my own advice into action tonight. I have dinner plans with a new Hindu friend from my gym, and I have high hopes of beginning to invest in her spiritually.

 CHAPTER 6

Ten Reasons Not to Disciple

"She just dropped off," Janet said as we talked in the hallway at a conference I was speaking at. "She said she wanted to be discipled, and I was excited to have someone to pour my life into, but it just didn't work out."

As I talked with Janet longer, it was clear that she was very disappointed. She had high hopes for this discipleship relationship, and at some point it fizzled into nothing. I asked questions such as, "How long had you known Jackie (the woman she had been discipling)? Was there good communication at the onset as to what you wanted to see happen in the discipleship relationship? Did you spend time with her consistently as a friend and as a discipler? Was she teachable? Was she connected to a larger body of believers than just you?" I was trying to diagnose what might have happened to give Janet some sort of clarity and help for the future.

For women who want to disciple another, it can be easy to ride on the initial enthusiasm of someone who wants and needs discipleship. We're prone to begin immediately discipling someone without waiting to see if that person has the qualities necessary to be a disciple at that stage in her life. And further there are some women who may begin to disciple a woman without being ready for such a responsibility themselves.

The rule of thumb is to not move too quickly. You need to take time to observe, pray and make an informed decision. You only have a certain number of hours in the day and a certain number of days in your life. We need to be good stewards of our time by discipling those who not only want to be discipled, but who will eventually (hopefully) go on to teach others. Listed below are ten of the most common reasons you might not want to disciple a particular person, starting with a few reasons focused on you as the discipler.

1. You Are Not Walking With God

Discipleship is not easy. It takes work, love, encouragement, and patience. It is a God-ordained relationship, and you will need the Lord to work through you in a powerful way. Sometimes, if I am feeling far from God, I take a day or half-day to focus on my relationship with Him.

I remember a morning (and into the afternoon) when I stayed in my pajamas for four hours reading old journals. I spent time praising God for all the answered prayers for the requests I found looking through those journals. I also grieved the petty struggles that had plagued me years ago that were still bothering me currently. Flipping through the pages of my journals reminded me of old friends, cherished memories, and significant lessons God had taught me throughout the years. By the end of the day, I felt renewed in my relationship with the Lord, and had a sense that God would answer my prayers. I was also renewed in my dedication to say no to sin and yes to righteousness; I wanted to be used by God in the lives of others.

I don't know what it would take for you to renew your relationship with God if you feel you are in a rut. It may take consistent prayer, fasting, a personal retreat, etc. But I do know this: If you are not moving forward in this relationship, it will be difficult to teach another how to do so in her life. For more on walking with God, see Chapter 2, "The Discipler and Her Relationship with God."

2. You Have Unconfessed Sin

We don't want to be hypocrites. If you're struggling in an area, you need to talk to the Lord about it, and then share it with someone else. I regularly share the things I'm going through with the women I am discipling. In addition to accountability partners, I have a dear friend named Shannon, who used to be my direct supervisor, with whom I have shared struggles throughout the years. It's important to note that unconfessed sin can give Satan a foothold in our lives and hinder our ability to lead others.

I recall one young woman I discipled years ago. She was in a continual struggle not to have sex with her boyfriend and remain pure. I remember her crying to me, saying, "How can I ask the women I'm discipling about their walk with God and with their boyfriends if I am involved in this?" Exactly — we need to overcome sin in our lives and confess it to others so we can minister with a clear conscience.

3. Not Enough Observation

Take your time; it is easy to want to start immediately discipling someone who seems so excited or needy, but you must observe people first. Make sure you are discipling people who are consistent, helpful, teachable, reliable, and faithful. If you rush to begin a discipleship relationship with a woman, you may move too quickly and regret it later, as I found out happened with Janet in the story that opened this chapter. We need to disciple women who can later reproduce growth in others. This is the key to developing individuals who can turn around and disciple others. Take your time, therefore, and choose wisely: "And the things you have heard me say in the presence of many witness, entrust to reliable men who will also be qualified to teach others" (2 Timothy 2:2, NIV). For more information on these characteristics see Chapter 3, "S.T.A.R.T. Discipling."

4. Hectic Schedule

If a woman is overcommitted and spread too thin, she will be unable to give a discipleship relationship priority and may not have time to disciple others in the future. When she is too busy with work, family, school, or sports activities, she may also be too busy for discipleship. I'm not saying people should cease every activity that does not involve discipleship or spiritual matters. However, limiting activities for a season to be discipled and to eventually disciple others is important. When I was in college, I found that a good rule of thumb is to be involved in both Christian and non-Christian activities.

For example, at Tyler Junior College, I was involved in the Baptist Student Union (a group of Christian college students) and the theater department. By limiting my activities, I had time to go to attend Bible study and be involved in Sunday school socials while still having time to be involved in theater productions and build relationships with people in the theater department. To maintain a flexible schedule, I elected not to be involved in intramural sports, the honor society, or a sorority. These would have been great activities, but they would have crowded out the time I needed to be discipled and build relationships with other women.

5. Not Committed to a Body of Believers

She doesn't attend church, home group, or anything besides her discipleship meetings with you. She expects you to teach her all she needs to know, but that is simply impossible. A woman needs to be committed to something larger than you. You don't have all the resources necessary to help her grow. She needs the larger body of Christ.

In many situations it would be ideal if both of you are involved in the same church or organization. This would enable you to steer her toward ideal situations for growth and further development. However, I know of many cases where the discipler and the disciple attend different churches or organizations. An example is my friend, Kay.

Kay is a mom of four, has an advanced degree in counseling, and is committed to world missions. She also has a burden for discipleship in the church. She regularly meets with a group of ladies from all over her city to teach them basic discipleship skills. Eventually they will turn around and disciple people in their own church bodies. Although not all the women come to her church, they will be able to reproduce what they have learned in their own home churches.

6. Professional Counseling Needed

There will be instances when someone's issues are far too complex for a discipleship relationship. She might have such deep emotional scars and issues that the best thing for her would be to see a professional counselor.

A number of years ago, Stephanie was a woman I had gotten to know as we lived close to each other. We were both single and would hang out every so often. She had become a Christian, and I wanted to help her grow in her new relationship with Christ. As I got to know her, however, she began to tell me of her frequent thoughts of suicide. Her mother had died when she was a young girl and her dad had raised her. From what I understood at that point, the dad had done a terrific job of raising her, however, thoughts of death and suicide lingered. Even though Stephanie was in the Bible study I led once a week, I knew I did not have the skills to help her to the extent she needed. I determined that the time we might have spent together in discipleship would be better spent by her in an appointment with a professional counselor.

You are welcome to walk alongside any woman going through a tough time with a certain issue in her life, but for some issues, women need professional counseling. For more on issues that need professional counseling, refer to Part II of this book.

7. Not Teachable

This woman insists on having it her way and is reluctant to listen or embrace any truth you might bring to her life. She may use excuses such as "That's just the way I am," "I can't help it," and "That's the way I was raised." This woman may become offended by correction instead of being thankful for your love and honesty. This is a big deal. How can a woman apply the Bible to her life if she is not willing to see any need for change? We need to be teachable ourselves — always looking for opportunities to grow, gain wisdom, embrace the advice of others. And we need to see this in the women we are discipling. If they are unteachable, you are going to come quickly to a brick wall in your relationship together.

8. Unreliable

If your disciple often stands you up, sleeps through the appointment, or plans to do something else, she is not reliable. If she fails to honor commitments, however trivial they may seem, she is not reliable. Committing to a discipleship relationship with this type of person will leave you feeling consistently frustrated. I discipled a girl for a while and she stood me up three times in a row. Each week I thought it would be different, but each week I was disappointed. I would ask her, "Is there another place or time you would like to meet?" or "Is there something you want to tell me?" But each week she had an excuse. The bummer was that there were other women desiring for someone to be in their life to help them and walk alongside them in discipleship, and here I was waiting week after week for my friend to show.

9. Involved in Blatant Sin

Okay, we are all sinners. I am not referring to a person who is ashamed of sin and continues to confess and seek God until she has victory, but rather someone who is perhaps living with her boyfriend and sees no problem with it, or who openly views pornography as a normal pastime. This is a person who, regardless of the issue, has embraced the sin rather than rejecting it and trying to gain victory over it. Until she is fully ready to confess the sin for what it is and is ready to ask for God's forgiveness and strength to overcome it, she is not ready to enter into a discipleship relationship. In these cases, the wisest thing you can do is to not disciple the woman, but rather allow God to work in her heart to bring conviction of sin.

10. Not Outreach-Oriented

"I just don't think I need to talk to people about God," Kristine said as we talked about sharing our faith in Christ with others. "They know I am a Christian and they can ask me if they have questions."

She also did not feel comfortable talking to visitors who came to Bible study or inviting people to church. It is normal to feel nervous when talking to others about Jesus. Certainly some people are not as outgoing as others. However, there is a difference between a shy personality and a staunch unwillingness take a step of faith in reaching out.

Help — I am already discipling a woman described in the list!

Don't panic! These women are deeply loved by God, and I would not want to come across as suggesting that you drop her. That would only hurt. Take some time to pray and pinpoint the specific issues that might be hindering her growth. Then plan to talk about those issues the next time you meet. The conversation could look something like this:

"Noelle, I enjoy our time together and had a blast with you at the '80s party this past weekend! You looked so funny! Before we jump in today, I wanted to share with you something I have observed that might hinder you in the long run. I have noticed a few times that when I ask you to do something, you either forget or have an excuse. I understand that things will come up and emergencies will happen, but I feel like this has become a weekly thing with you. For example, I waited 45 minutes last week for you to show up to our discipleship appointment. You said you had forgotten we'd planned to meet. The week before I waited 30 minutes for you, and you said you were late because you needed to run an errand. It's getting to the point where I doubt you will show up, and I don't feel I can depend on you. Noelle, I know you don't want to be like this; I know your heart is to be dependable. I just want to take a good look at this today and talk about what needs to change." For more on having hard conversations, see Chapter 8, "Speaking the Truth in Love."

If something from the list in this chapter is already taking place, take some time to dialogue with your disciple about it. Talk about possible solutions and ideas that might help. Remember, you are doing her a huge favor by talking about the issues openly and not making excuses. As in the case above, she will not be able to keep a job with that type of unreliability, and it could hinder her relationships with others besides you.

Under Construction

All of us are in process. If you have put your faith in Christ and are seeking to grow in your relationship with Him, you are in a sanctifying process. So are others. Just because someone might not be an immediate candidate for discipleship does not mean she will never be ready to be discipled. Make sure, therefore, that you do not write off someone completely. Let God have His way in her life and bring her to a point where she is eager to be discipled and grow spiritually.

Begin With the End in Mind

It's always a good idea to know where you are going before you begin. You don't want to meet with a disciple just to meet with her; you want to have a goal in mind. The first goal is for her to look more and more like Jesus each day by developing a closer walk with Him. It would also be terrific if she learning some basic ministry skills. To help you reach that goal, it is helpful to have a few tangible plans in mind.

I remember early on as a director of local campus ministry with Cru (formerly Campus Crusade for Christ), I wanted to disciple my new staff members to eventually be campus directors themselves. Each time I planned for our appointment, I would think about what they would need to know to be a campus director. For example, I wanted them to know not only how to study the Bible, but also how to teach someone else to study the Bible. I wanted them not only to be able to share their faith, but also teach others to share their faith. When I met with my young students, I wanted them each to eventually disciple another person and lead a Bible study. So when I planned for my discipleship appointments, I would include a portion of time to address these issues. In this way, my goals for them helped me to plan my appointments with them.

Spend time thinking through clear goals for each woman you are disci- pling. What do you want the end goal to be? I've found that beginning with the end in mind helps me as I plan each week. Goals and well- thought-out development plans help me make sure that I cover all the bases of their training and discipleship. It's a thrill to see all the women who have gone on to lead Bible studies, teach others to share their faith, or direct ministries.

100 vs. 10

"Do you want to partner with 100 people who are 10 percent committed or 10 people who are 100 percent committed?"

I am not sure where I first read this question, but it is burned onto the hard drive of my mind. I want to disciple people who are 100 percent committed to growing and helping fulfill the Great Commission. I would rather disciple a few people who are completely committed than hundreds who are only half-hearted. I do, though, want to make the distinction that they don't have to be 100 percent perfect — just 100 percent willing.

We don't have time to disciple people who don't really want to be discipled, or who just don't want to grow. I have a desire to help fulfill the Great Commission. Since you are reading this book, I bet you do as well. If you spend your time discipling people who are not ready to be discipled, they will not be eager to pass along the information you are teaching. Without this continuing chain of knowledge, fewer people will have the opportunity to be discipled and grow. You want to disciple those who are ready to give God their all, take steps of faith, and eventually disciple others. I do not wish to imply that the person must be a perfect Christian. If that were the case, I certainly could not disciple anyone. I only wish to emphasize that we need to choose wisely and disciple women who will help us reach others.

In Summary

There are a variety of factors that signal that a woman is not ready to be discipled. Women should be encouraged to continue their involvement in a bible study and church but since you have limited time and resources, you need to choose wisely who to disciple. Keep in mind that discipling only a few women who are totally committed to growing and taking steps of faith in their walk with God will be better in the long run than discipling many women who are only half-hearted concerning discipleship and maturing in their walk with God.

 CHAPTER 7

Commitment to Discipleship

Not again, I thought as I sat at the table glancing at my watch every few minutes. Surely she is not going to be late again. Everything was ready to go, and with each passing minute I was getting more and more frustrated. Laura had consistently been arriving late to our discipleship appointments, and on one occasion she had stood me up completely. Whenever I tried to call, her phone would go straight to voice mail. We'd already had several conversations concerning this. I'd inquired several times if she had too much on her plate or was overwhelmed in life, but she never indicated that she was overwhelmed and always apologized with an excuse. I patiently explained to Laura that I spent time carefully planning what we'd do together. This plan hinged on a timely start of the appointment, and it hurt my feelings that she did not prioritize the time as I had. I thought those conversations had taken care of the problem. Yet here I was again glancing at my watch, watching the door, and waiting for her. I sat there mentally adjusting our schedule as our allotted time quickly ran out. How would I tell her that I didn't want to do this anymore if she was not going to begin putting more effort into it?

In discipleship, a myriad of situations can arise where you might have to end a discipleship relationship. Situations can range from skipped appointments to unrepentant sin, a seeming decline in interest, or a complete withdrawal from the church. These situations can be painful and sometimes heartbreaking.

A few helpful tools can be used at the front end of a new discipleship relationship to give both women a clear understanding of discipleship and its expectations. They are a simple Bible study lesson and commitment sheet that both women read together.

"Counting the Cost" Bible Study

I'd been meeting and spending time regularly with Brooke ever since she had trusted Christ as her Lord and Savior earlier that year. After we finished some basic material designed for a new believer, I began to think about the next step. "Brooke, I'd like for us to continue meeting together," I said, "but before we move forward, it's a good idea for us both to have a clear understanding of what the commitment will entail on both our parts. I would like to work through a short Bible study with you to learn what Jesus taught about counting the cost before making a commitment." I pulled out the following Bible study:

BIBLE STUDY | COUNTING THE COST

Read Luke 14:25-35

Questions for Understanding:

What do you think Jesus means when he says, "If anyone comes to me and does not hate his father and mother, his wife and children, his brothers and sisters-yes, even his own life-he cannot be my disciple"?

What is the first thing the tower builder should do before he begins to build?

What is the first thing the King does before he goes to war?

What do you think is the main point Jesus is trying to get across?

Why do you think he had such demanding requirements?

Personal Application:

Is there a relationship that hinders, obstructs, or takes precedence over your devotion to Christ?

Are you willing to submit/yield your dreams and plans for the future to the will of God?

What dreams are most difficult for you to yield to God?

Are you willing to narrow your activities and involvement to enable you to be available for discipleship?

Jesus concludes his discourse by saying, "He who has ears let him hear." In other words, Jesus respected His followers' individuality by giving them the choice. Many of those who chose to become his disciples were probably among the group of 120 who responded to Jesus' challenge (Acts 1:15). Perhaps others made that choice later. Most certainly, some never made the choice at all.

What will you do?

An Eternal Perspective:

"Show me, O Lord, my life's end and the number of my days; let me know how fleeting is my life. You have made my days a mere handbreadth; the span of my years is as nothing before you. Each man's life is but a breath." Psalm 39:4-6

BIBLE STUDY | COUNTING THE COST (continued)

(note: Handbreadth-is one of the smallest units of measurement in ancient Israel. It is the equivalent of a couple of inches. Thus the psalmist reminds himself that life is short.)

Calculating the Benefits:

By being committed to a discipleship relationship, ask yourself...

How will I benefit now? How will I benefit in the future? How will I benefit in eternity?

"I want to free up time to embrace the only things that will last anyway." *Personal Disciplemaking*, Chris Adsit, pg. 17.

(Some information for this Bible study adapted from the Interacta lesson "The Price is Right")

Brooke and I began to read through the lesson together. We turned to Luke 14:25-35, she and I read aloud the following passage:

"Large crowds were traveling with Jesus, and turning to them he said: "If anyone comes to me and does not hate his father and mother, his wife and children, his brothers and sisters-yes, even his own life-he cannot be my disciple. And anyone who does not carry his cross to follow me cannot be my disciple.

"Suppose one of you wants to build a tower. Will he not first sit down and estimate the cost to see if he has enough money to complete it? For if he lays the foundation and is not able to finish it, everyone who sees it will ridicule him, saying, 'This fellow began to build and was not able to finish.'

"Or suppose a king is about to go to war against another king. Will he not first sit down and consider whether he is able with ten thousand men to oppose the one coming against him with twenty thousand? If he is not able, he will send a delegation while the other is still a long way off and will ask for terms of peace. In the same way, any of you who does not give up everything he has cannot be my disciple."

"Salt is good, but if it loses its saltiness, how can it be made salty again? It is fit neither for the soil nor for the manure pile; it is thrown out."

"He who has ears let him hear" (NIV).

We then went over questions dealing with both the passage in general and personal application. Brooke needed to understand that she herself would need to count the cost when it came to following Christ.

After our discussion, Brooke indicated that she was willing to count the cost and submit her plans to the will of God. She was willing to follow the Holy Spirit's leading in her life, whatever that may be. I told her I was proud of her. I shared some of the dreams and plans I'd yielded to God throughout the years, including dreams of being an actress and of being married. I encouraged her to trust God to lead her along the best pathway for her life. "Brooke," I said, "God loves us and has created us for a purpose and a destiny. Only by following after Him and putting our plans at the foot of His throne will we fulfill the purposes for which He created us."

The Discipleship Commitment Sheet

"Brooke," I continued, "this discipleship relationship will require a commitment on both our parts. I'd like to read and talk through this sheet together." As Brooke was a member of the Cru Bible study I led, I had specifically made this commitment sheet to reflect her involvement in our ministry.

DISCIPLESHIP | THE COMMITMENT

If you were embarking on an enterprise of great significance, would you rather partner with one hundred people who were 10% committed, or ten people who are 100% committed? Why?

My commitment to you...

- Pray consistently for and with you
- Spend regular one-on-one time with you
- Be available to you
- Train you in the basics of walking with God and ministry skills
- Ask the hard questions
- Communicate truth in grace and love

Your commitment...

- Attend a Bible study and invite friends
- Attend one conference/ retreat this year
- Attend discipleship appointment each week
- Commitment to a local church

Heart Issues

- Filled with the Holy Spirit
- Receptive to correction
- Keep short accounts
- Transparent
- Others-focused
- Spend time with Jesus
- Consistent prayer life
- Willingness to share Christ with others

Heart Issues

I've found over time that a woman can do the right things and meet certain criteria, but her heart may be far from the Lord. That's why this commitment sheet lists heart issues. I certainly wouldn't want a woman to just do good things, such as attend Bible study or attend conferences, while neglecting her heart. When I go through this commitment sheet with a person, we spend the majority of our time on this section. I am very concerned that she be filled with the Holy Spirit, keep short accounts with God concerning her sin, and have a willing heart to reach out to others.

Making Adjustments

Feel free to adjust this commitment sheet to make it a useful tool for you and your ministry. For example, if I were a youth director, I would change the commitment sheet to read, "Attend youth group each Wednesday, come to church on Sunday, attend socials and fun nights, and bring friends." When I disciple people from my church, I change the sheet to say, "Attend church service regularly, invite friends to home group, and try to participate in one outreach this year."

The Next Step

After I've met with a woman for over a year, or if she was mature in her walk with God when I met her, I would use a similar discipleship challenge, but her commitment would be a bit more faith-stretching.

Advantages

There are many advantages to using the commitment sheet. First, it gives both women a clear understanding and foundation upon which to build the discipleship relationship. Second, it can serve as a challenge toward which the disciple can strive. Third, when the disciple begins to disciple others, she will know very clearly what her role will be as the discipler. Furthermore, as was the case with Laura at the beginning of this chapter, the sheet can serve as a commitment reminder.

That day, when Laura finally did show up, I pulled out the commitment form we had walked through earlier that year. I gently talked with her about her ongoing tardiness and absence issues. I told her, "Laura, I'd like for us to read back through this commitment sheet together and re-evaluate whether or not this is a good season for you to be in a discipleship relationship." This type of conversation can be very difficult. If she no longer wants to embrace her part of the commitment, the disciple simply removes herself from the relationship.

I certainly would not threaten to stop discipling a woman after a few strikes. The commitment sheet is not intended to be a weapon. Discipleship shouldn't be a harsh, perfectionist type of relationship. However, reality is that in past discipleship relationships, I've had women who, for one reason or another, have stopped meeting with me. I would not look to end a relationship with a woman going through a difficult time, if she is doing her best to actively work through sin in her life. I would, however, take a close look at a woman who does not prioritize the appointment, is not involved in a larger fellowship, or is living with unrepentant sin. In each of these cases, I'd make it clear that I would be open to reinstating the discipleship as soon as circumstances change.

Remember the Cost

At times, my disciples or I must be reminded that there is an opportunity cost and a commitment involved in discipleship. There is a cost when I say no to a fun opportunity in order to arrive at my appointment on time, when I call one of my girls and pray with her even when I am tired, or when I wake up early to plan for discipleship appointments. If over time, a woman in a discipleship relationship is not willing to count the cost, it is going to leave the other frustrated and hurt. I've found that clear expectations are an asset, not a hindrance.

Not Too Late

It is not too late to implement this type of formalized commitment into your discipleship relationships. Even if you have been meeting with a woman for a long time, copy this commitment sheet, modifying it to better reflect your ministry or situation, and begin implementing it in your relationships.

In Summary

Tools such as the "Counting the Cost" Bible study and the commitment sheet outline a clear and concrete understanding of expectations involved in discipleship relationships. This is beneficial to both parties, especially when situations arise that call for a re-evaluation of the relationship. Just the other day, a woman I discipled a few years ago emailed me asking for a copy of these materials. They were so helpful to her when she and I began our discipleship relationship that she wanted to use them with a woman she was beginning to disciple.

 **CHAPTER 8**

Speaking the Truth in Love

I was on a summer-long mission trip in the Middle East when Linda, one of the project directors and my ministry partner, approached me.

"Lori, there are a few things I'd like to talk to you about," Linda said.

"Sure," I said, "what's up?"

"Lori, you've been so fun to partner with on this trip. Your boldness for Christ and flexible personality are great assets to our team."

"Thanks," I said, feeling rather proud of myself.

"I have noticed a few things, though," Linda continued, "that I wanted to bring to your attention and talk about this afternoon. When we all get together at night and talk about our day, you have a habit of interrupting when someone else is talking. And often you talk all about yourself and things you have done without really listening to others and asking about their lives."

Whoa! I was not expecting that. Linda talked with me at length over this. I was quite upset, even though everything she said was true. I remember retorting through my tears, "Are you going to go tell all the other girls their problems?!"

Linda handled things calmly and compassionately. After telling me how much she cared for me, she left my room. I sat on my bed and cried, hurt but knowing what she had said was true. I wrote in my journal and asked God to help me become more others-centered and less me-centered. Over time, God has helped me become interested in other people, listen when they speak, and genuinely care about what is going on in their lives. That conversation with Linda has had a significant impact on my current ministry. Being able to focus on others and challenge them to grow in Christ, rather than being self-consumed, has helped me be a better discipler and friend.

I am certain it was not easy for Linda to talk to me about what she'd observed. I know this from experience. When I've needed to confront women about issues in their lives, it's always been hard for me. It takes a step of faith and involves risk. Below are a few fundamental items you need to grasp before you confront a disciple or friend about an issue. These items are not in any particular order; each is an important element to speaking the truth in love.

The Fundamentals

1. Pray

Pray that God would help you speak in a graceful, loving way. You don't want your approach to be harsh or condemning, but compassionate and kind. Also, pray that God would prepare her heart to receive what you have to say.

2. Face to Face

Wait to address the issue during your regular discipleship time. You don't want to call her and blurt out the issue over the phone. Talking with a woman face to face enables you to read her body language. Plus, she has already carved out that time to meet with you, so it is neither inconvenient nor rushed. This is not something you want to hurry through. Make sure you have enough time to discuss it thoroughly.

3. Deposits and Withdrawals

Make sure you've made deposits in her emotional bank by affirming her before you make a withdrawal through a confrontation. This means you need to love and encourage her constantly. You must be this woman's main cheerleader! You must shower praise on her and consistently tell her that you are proud of her. These deposits add up in her emotional bank so that when you have to make a withdrawal by means of hard conversation, the relationship can handle it.

4. Multiple Issues

Avoid addressing multiple issues at once. For example, if I told you that you constantly interrupt people, you are not dependable, and gossip excessively about others, you would feel not only hurt, but probably also overwhelmed. As a discipler, take time to observe and determine the root issue that may be driving other issues. Focus on one issue at a time.

5. Committed to Growth

Your motivation in confronting a disciple should be love, grace, and her continued growth. You want her to know, even if she is initially hurt, that you love her and are not trying to hurt her. Emphasize that you want her to thrive and to disciple others herself in the future. Be quick to say that you have only her best in mind and reassure her that you brought this up only because it was absolutely necessary for her continued growth.

Sample Segues

Remember to begin your time with affirmation. Affirm her in a specific way. You could, for example, tell her you're proud of some recent step of faith, of her readiness to learn, or of the single act of bringing a spiritually lost friend to church. Then segue into the truth, always speaking in love. Here are a few ways to begin this challenging conversation:

If you have been discipling the woman for a few months, you might say, "Since we've begun meeting for discipleship and getting to know each other, there's something I've noticed that I wanted to bring to your attention. It's hard for me to bring this up because I care about you and don't want to hurt your feelings. However, because I'm committed to your growth in every area of life, I didn't want to put off talking about this with you. Over the past _____ (time period) I've noticed that you_____ (fill in the blank)."

If the person is in a leadership position of some sort, you could say, "In light of the fact that you are leading women, I'd like to submit something to you. It's hard for me to speak truth sometimes because I risk hurting you, but because I love you, it's worth it to me to come to you. Over the past _____ (time period) I've noticed that you_____ (fill in the blank)."

Be Specific

Remember to share a specific example to help the woman understand what you're talking about. For example, you don't want to say, "You talk too much," because that is too vague. Instead say, "I have noticed that in home group, when we are having a discussion, you seem to be quick to answer all the questions and share lengthy stories to the point that others don't have the opportunity to talk as well."

Be specific as you talk. Whatever the issue is, it will be a challenging conversation. But skirting around the real issue won't help her. It will likely confuse her more.

Help Her Change

I remember talking with Cheryl about the critical way she spoke to others. I reminded her of a recent incident in which we brainstormed for an upcoming event. At one point she replied to another woman's comment with, "That's a stupid idea." I gently explained that she could have either suggested a different idea or said nothing at all. It is not enough to just tell them the truth; help them make the necessary changes. If the woman talks constantly in a group settings, have her consider asking two questions of others for every one story she tells about herself. The bottom line is to help her figure out ways to change.

When to Confront

Do not confront a woman until these criteria have been met. If you jump too soon, you'll regret it later, the reason being that you may hurt the woman in the long run instead of helping her. If one of the criteria is missing, perhaps it's not the Lord's timing, or you haven't taken time to really figure out the root issue. Or perhaps you have the problem, not her. Remember, do not confront unless:

* You've prayed about the issue and for the woman

* Your motivation is love, grace, and her continued growth

* You can clearly identify a specific problem

* You have at least one specific example to back up your concern

* You're ready to help her change

A Few Extras

Be quick to give personal examples of people speaking truth into your life and how you felt at the time ("I remember the time my first Bible study leader talked to me about the clothes I was wearing. I felt ..."). I often tell the story I told at the beginning the chapter and how Linda's words to me on that mission trip affected me. Be vulnerable.

End your time in prayer, and set a time for the two of you to get together for fun. She needs to know that she hasn't let you down or fallen from your favor. Whether you watch a movie, exercise, or grab lunch on your break together, be intentional about spending time with her.

There may be times when the woman is so shocked by your words that she may be unable to respond. At your next discipleship appointment, you may need to bring up the subject again and ask if she has any additional thoughts or questions.

In Summary

When discipling women, there will be times when you notice something in their lives that calls for special attention. As the discipler, you are responsible for helping them see the issue and make necessary changes. Your motivation needs to be her continued growth.

Being confronted with blind spots in my life has helped me grow, mature, and minister to others more effectively. This is a necessary part of discipleship relationships — or any friendships, for that matter. Don't put off talking with someone and speaking the truth in love. They'll thank you for it later, just as I have thanked Linda numerous times.

 **CHAPTER 9**

Cross-Cultural Discipleship

When I walked into my Tuesday evening Bible study, I smiled as I thought about the difference between these students and those who typically attended my mostly white Bible studies. That Tuesday evening my own blonde hair and light complexion was quite a contrast to the other women, all of whom were African Americans. A new release by MaryMary, a popular African-American Christian artist, was playing, and the women were dancing and teaching each other new steps and moves … moves that on my best day I could never replicate. They tried to teach me, but I suspect it was because my attempts were so entertaining. They chatted and laughed as they caught up on each other's day over refreshments.

In the course of the study that evening, there were several lively discussions. These women were passionate about certain issues, and they shared hard experiences with genuine transparency. Several times I leaned over to ask Nikkea, my co-leader, to explain a phrase or word I hadn't heard before, like "dropping it like it's hot," which I discovered refers to a dance move. Our prayer time was punctuated with sobs and groans as the women poured out heartache and hard family times.

Later, I thought about the fact that I'd never started a Bible study with dancing, and I couldn't remember attending or leading a Bible study where I didn't understand the terms and phrases being used. Tuesday night, however, was only the beginning of what would become a grand new adventure.

I've ministered to students from different ethnic backgrounds since 1998, when God began an amazing work among African-American students on the university campus where I served as a Cru staff person. Since that time, many Hispanic and Asian students have become involved in the Cru ministry at the university. As resident director of a ministry home for female students for four years, I lived with Asian Americans, Hispanic Americans, and African Americans. That hasn't made me an expert in cross-cultural ministry; I'm still a learner. However, since being initiated into cross-cultural ministry in '98, I've learned a few things that have been helpful.

Maybe a few of these principles and observations will be helpful to you.

Why Cross-Cultural?

First, we disciple cross-culturally because Jesus instructed us to go and make disciples of all nations (Matthew 28:18-20). Matthew recorded those words of Jesus, but he didn't say how he and the other disciples responded to the part about all nations. Given the disciples' initial reluctance to carry news of Jesus the Messiah outside Judaism, we can imagine that they didn't grasp the all nations part right away. Perhaps that's why Jesus, alone with the disciples on the Mount of Olives ten days after His crucifixion, phrased the instruction another way: "But you will receive power when the Holy Spirit comes on you; and you will be my witnesses in Jerusalem, and in all Judea and Samaria, and to the ends of the earth" (Acts 1:8, NIV).

Jerusalem was the hometown of several of the disciples, Judea was the surrounding province, Samaria was the province contiguous to Judea's northern border, and "the ends of the earth" was the whole world. Bible scholars suggest the Acts 1 passage is a model for evangelizing and discipling — we start at home, then expand to the surrounding area, not stopping until we reach the ends of the earth.

Clearly, Jesus intended that His followers evangelize and disciple across every culture. In Acts 10, Peter reached across his Jewish culture into the Roman culture to explain the gospel to Cornelius and his household. In his first missionary journey (Acts 13:4–14:28), Paul ministered to both Jews and Gentiles, and on the second journey (Acts 15:39–18:22) he practiced what for a first-century Jew was the ultimate cross-cultural ministry: he ministered to the Areopagus, the court of Greek philosophers in Athens.

Another reason to disciple cross-culturally is that we inevitably become more effective in all cultures. As we evangelize and disciple persons from other countries and cultures, we intuitively begin deleting all the cultural baggage that has been attached to the message.

Many of the world's nations are represented here in America. In fact, given America's world position, there's a sense in which Judea, Samaria, and the ends of the earth have come to us. Seeing this on college campuses, in neighborhoods, at gyms and in the grocery store, we can no longer be content only reaching out to people who look like us. We can be about the business of Matthew 28 by reaching out right around us. Furthermore, the ethnic population in America is growing rapidly; if we don't evangelize and disciple that growing part of our country, we'll miss sharing the gospel with a large percentage of our population.

If we're serious about reaching every person for Christ, we must cross boundaries and disciple persons who will become effective disciplers in their own cultures. Jesus is the way, the truth and the life for all people, regardless of race or ethnicity. As we fall more in love with Him, we will see His compassion for every nation, people, tribe, and tongue, and we will yearn to share that compassion.

Over the past several years I've found that the highlight of my ministry is when I'm reaching out to other cultures. The opportunity to learn about different traditions, foods, humor, and perspectives while seeing that Scripture applies to all of us is something you don't want to miss out on!

Contextualization is Key

As Lucia entered the Bible Study sponsored by Destino, a ministry designed to reach Hispanic students, she immediately felt at home. The snacks were typical of her culture, the music was Spanish, and the examples used to apply Scripture to life were ones she could easily relate to. Lucia, like many other students, was attracted to the fact that this Bible study was familiar to her. Furthermore, the roadblocks to learning about Christ had been totally eliminated.

In cross-cultural discipleship, it is essential to keep contextualization in mind. According to the Ethnic Student Ministries School of Leadership, each culture has three groups: assimilated, bi-cultural, and contextualized.

A person who is assimilated is immersed in the dominant culture, where he or she feels most comfortable. For example, a female Asian-American student who is most comfortable in the white culture around her may have grown up in an all-white neighborhood, possibly attended a (predominantly) white school, and may be active in an all-white church. She is assimilated.

If that same person also feels at home with other Asian Americans, has many Asian-American friends, understands Asian humor and likes Asian food, she's bi-cultural. That is, she feels at home in either the white or Asian culture.

We would say she is contextualized if she typically prefers Asian-American settings — perhaps she grew up in an Asian section of his city, attended a largely Asian school, or only shopped at grocery stores serving Asian cuisine.

All populations include these three types. I am a white bi-cultural female, which means I'm comfortable in my own culture, attended a mostly white school, etc. But I'm also comfortable attending African-American churches and living with people of different ethnicities. I'm sure ministering to other cultures on several overseas trips helped me become bi-cultural here at home.

In order to effectively disciple someone cross-culturally, it's important to know if your student is assimilated, bi-cultural, or contextualized; this knowledge will shape your approach throughout the discipleship process.

Our mostly white ministries will reach assimilated students of all cultures since they're comfortable with white, American customs. We may also reach some bi-cultural students. However, our white ministries likely will not reach contextualized students. It is therefore imperative to keep contextualization in mind as we begin new ministries and disciple ethnic students.

I remember asking Hannah, an African-American student I discipled, to meet me at Common Grounds, a well-known coffee shop by our campus. "What's that?" she asked. "You know — Common Grounds," I said. After I explained that Common Grounds was the name of a coffee shop, she said the reason she hadn't known about it was that African Americans don't hang out in coffee shops like white people do. (Since this conversation — and the boom of a Starbucks on every corner — this has changed. At the time, however, going to a coffee shop was foreign to Hannah.)

It was much more comfortable for her to meet in the student union building, which in my opinion wasn't very comfortable. There are no big, cushy chairs, and the coffee isn't as good as that at Common Grounds, but we met there because I wanted her to feel comfortable. I wanted to eliminate any barriers to her learning. I'm willing to put myself in un-comfortable situations so that the women I disciple do not feel required to conform to my ways. I wanted Hannah to be a leader in her culture, not mine, so I walked to the student union building and greeted her with a big smile.

Be a Student of Your Disciple

I sat across from Karen, an Asian American, who looked worn down and tired. "Why the long face?" I asked. "Oh, nothing, she replied. "I'm just busy and I feel like there aren't enough hours in the day to get things done." As we talked, I asked about her activities and schedule.

It amazed me to see all she was doing. She led worship for a weekly gathering, discipled three women, led a coed Bible study, met weekly with me for discipleship, and worked at Starbucks. All that was in addition to her graduate classes and her responsibility as a graduate assistant. Just listening to her made me tired!

I was just beginning to learn about Asian cultures and their approach to authority figures. I began to realize how difficult it is for Asian-American students to say no. Karen and I talked about her habit of agreeing to do anything asked of her. She explained that she had never said no to her parents, and now, since she wasn't saying no to me, I had enlisted her for all sorts of tasks. They were important jobs, but not important enough that they should cause Karen to eventually experience burnout.

I was accustomed to white students declining a new responsibility if their schedules were full; I knew if they couldn't handle the load, they'd just say so. Because she always said yes and did things so well, other people also delegated tasks to Karen. This constant burden of being loaded with tasks was pushing Karen to the point of circuit overload. And sadly, I was unaware. The cultural background that made it okay for me to call on her as a get-it-done person, compounded by the cultural background that didn't allow her to say no, created a hard situation until I stopped long enough to be a student of my disciple.

There are, of course, exceptions to what I've learned; I am not saying this is true of every Asian American. But as I began learning about Karen, I encouraged her to start saying no. I explained that she needed to become more assertive in saying no to me and others for her own sake. In fact, as an assignment, I asked that she say no to someone before we met again. I talked with others in my ministry that I worked with who also knew Karen, telling them what I was learning. I asked them not to delegate tasks to her until she could gain the strength and experience to say no when appropriate. Karen had grown up in a culture that respects authority to the degree that it had created unhealthy boundaries, or rather the absence of boundaries, in her life.

Karen and I also talked about this from a scriptural standpoint. Even though perpetual acquiescence might be normal in her culture, she needed to say no to some things in order to say yes to the right things. God had a plan and destiny for her life, and she needed to have the freedom to say yes to the things God had for her instead of all the favors others asked of her.

Being a student of your disciple means understanding her culture and the unique situations that will arise in your discipleship relationship. Learn about her family, traditions, holidays, and authority structures; ask lots of questions. Ask yourself, "Is this something she does consciously, or is it a result of some tradition or cultural norm?" My experience has taught me that I can't effectively minister to Asian-American women without understanding the role their family and parents play in their lives, and the resulting set of unique circumstances and situations brought into the discipleship relationship.

Culture and Sin

The phone rang early one morning, and Tiffany, an African-American woman I was discipling, was in tears: "Lori, I might get kicked out of my apartment if I don't come up with $400." She frantically told me that her landlord was threatening to kick her out if she didn't pay her rent. A bill she thought had already cleared her checking account months ago had just cleared her account, leaving her short on rent. As I listened and consoled her, I discovered that she was not keeping accurate records of her expenditures and hence was spending money she didn't have. She began blaming her landlord for being demanding, the bank for cashing the check too quickly, and so on. Tiffany grew up in a household where funds were limited and it was common to live from late notice to late notice. Because of a lack of education in this area, she saw no problem with paying bills late and owing people money as a way of life.

When trying to understand if an issue is cultural or sinful, you need to dig deep and ask good questions. Possibly the issue at hand is not a cultural issue but more of a generational sin issue. It could be a mix of both.

As I meet and disciple women from different ethnicities, I want to make sure I am not excusing sin by writing it off as a cultural difference. In other words, when I see a repeated pattern in any culture, I might have the tendency to say, "Well, this is just how it is in this culture, so I need to work around it." However, I have to keep in mind that I am not helping them when I excuse sin as just culture. Every culture has its issues. Cultural practices that don't line up with Scripture need to be addressed as sin, while keeping in mind that many cultural practices are amoral and hence are mere matters of taste and tradition.

I talked at length with Tiffany that morning, sharing grace and truth. I told her how sorry I was and explained that I knew what it meant not to have enough money to make ends meet (having bounced checks in college, I could relate). I also explained that her financial behavior did not line up with Scripture. I led her to James 5:12: "…let your yes be yes and your no be no …" — if she committed to pay rent, she needed to do it and stop blaming her landlord for expecting the payment on time. I also explained the necessity of her paying: other people have their own bills and need her money to do it — money she committed to paying when she signed the lease, set up the account, bought the car, etc.

Did I help her financially? Yes. I loved her and my heart went out to her. Did I pay the entire thing? No. I loaned her some of the money for three weeks and told her that when she paid it back, I wanted to see her check register balanced and in order. Instead of dismissing sin as just a cultural issue, use it as a way to teach biblical wisdom.

Getting Started

If you desire to begin discipling women of other ethnicities, the first thing to do is to put yourself in situations and places to meet women who are different than yourself. Monica Smith, a dear friend of mine, is a great example of this. Monica is a Caucasian committed to cross-cultural discipleship. She joined an African-American gospel choir. She didn't know anyone in the choir when she first showed up. Week after week she began to make friends and pray that God would use her in this choir in a significant way. Monica ended up meeting and discipling a young student named Kim. This same student became one of our first leaders of a ministry specifically designed to reach African-American students with the gospel.

Another way to get started is to conduct a focus group. A focus group is an evangelistic strategy that gathers women and asks them questions on a variety of topics such as the purpose of life, relationships, and spiritual issues. The focus group becomes a way to meet women and get to know them. This strategy can be done in a variety of different contexts including high schools, colleges, businesses, and neighborhoods. Monica and I first tried this strategy on a residence hall at a nearby college. She and I went up and down the floors taking surveys to invite women to this focus group. Monica and I were intentional about seeking out relationships with women of other ethnicities. The night of the focus group, we celebrated that we were the minority! We led a young woman to faith in Christ from that group and began to build relationships with the others as well.

Each and every ethnicity and people group need to hear the good news of Jesus Christ. You will have to be intentional about this; you can't wait for people to come to you. You must go to them. The Great Commission asks that the believer go to all who need to hear. It is a "go tell" and not a "come hear" command.

Go Deep With a Few

"Hi, Jenny," I said as I answered my cell phone.

"Lori, I have so many questions for you about a new ethnic ministry I have started. There are so many women that need to be discipled that I feel overwhelmed. I don't have the time to meet with them all."

For the next two hours I emphasized repeatedly that the best thing she can do is to go deep with only a few rather than spread herself too thin.

Jesus is our perfect model in this. Although he had twelve disciples, the Gospels constantly remind us of His special relationship with Peter, James, and John. These were the men who went up the mountain with Jesus to see the Transfiguration (Matthew 17:2). It was John who leaned on Jesus at the Last Supper (John 13:23-25), and Peter to whom Jesus gave the command to feed His sheep (John 21:15). Likewise, it is best to invest deeply with just a few and let multiplication spread from those few. Even though you are stepping out in faith and discipling cross-culturally, remember that you may not be as effective in their culture as they will be if they are discipled, loved, and trained well.

Be thorough in your discipleship of these women. Don't leave any stone unturned. Begin with the basics of walking with God, such as certainty of one's salvation, spending time alone with God, and the role of the Holy Spirit in one's life. Regarding ministry skills, begin by teaching how to communicate one's personal testimony, the gospel, and the ministry of the Holy Spirit as it relates to the Lordship of Christ in a person's life. Model everything well, and slowly transfer responsibility to the disciple. Give good feedback and constructive criticism at every turn. Offer encouragement and cast vision for how God will use her uniquely in her culture.

A Few Extras

Remember to be yourself. Don't try to be something you're not. It's fine if you don't understand the same lingo, dress similarly, frequent the same stores, or share identical musical tastes as the women you minister to. Be yourself; be the person God created you to be. Don't spend time trying to conform to another culture. Spend your time pursuing Christ and desiring to look and act more like Him. "Lori, you did not try to be like someone you were not," Casondra, a young African-American woman, replied when I asked her about our discipleship relationship and the things that stood out to her. "You were Lori, and you were secure in that. You didn't come into Bible study saying, 'Waz up dawg — I'm straight chillin'. Let's meet on the cut for discipleship.' You were just you, and the fact that you desired to help me grow in the Lord was what mattered the most."

Be quick to laugh at yourself. Some of the funniest things have happened in cross-cultural ministry. I remember the time some African-American women asked what my middle name was and I said, "Gerre" (pronounced Ja-REE). And they laughed till they cried as they told me I was meant to work with African-Americans with that middle name. Years ago they gave me my "black" name: Lorisha. And now, many years later, I am positive that the younger African-American women in that Bible study don't even know my real name.

When unsure about a cultural norm, ask about it plainly instead of being scared to offend. In writing this chapter I have called some of the women I have discipled cross-culturally to ask them questions so as to ensure that I represent them and their culture accurately and clearly. When you recognize and respect the cultural differences in those whom you disciple, you will have a greater doorway into their lives. So ask if unsure.

In Summary

To me, cross-cultural discipleship has been a special gift from God. It is a joy that is indescribable. I don't think I could have lasted this long in ministry had I not begun to disciple and become involved in ministries comprised of a variety of cultures. While this chapter merely scratches the surface of cross-cultural discipleship, my hope is that the information will be a helpful starting point for you in beginning to cross those cultural boundaries and to disciple women of different ethnicities.

 **CHAPTER 10**

Material for Growth

"Lori, what do I do now?" Lacy asked. We were at the mall shopping, and she'd just told me that her friend from work to whom she'd been witnessing had put her faith in Christ. "I don't know what to do next and I don't want to mess this up!"

"Don't worry Lacy, I'll walk through this with you," I said. "What do you think would be helpful to know for a woman who has just put her faith in Christ?"

"Well," Lacy answered, "I guess it would be good for her to know that if she messes up, she's still a Christian. And I should probably buy her a Bible, and maybe we should talk about going to church."

"Those are all great things to talk about with her. We'll brainstorm some more, and you can go through these topics each week when you get together."

Knowing where to begin with a new believer or a new disciple doesn't have to be stressful. If you take some time to think through what would be helpful, you'll probably do a pretty good job figuring out what to teach her. This chapter is dedicated to helping you think through some good topics to cover with your disciple, a few helpful resources, and an easy way to begin to write your own discipleship lessons.

Categories

As you get to know the woman you are discipling, you'll be able to see areas in her life you could address to help her grow. One way to think about possible topics to teach your disciple is to think in categories, such as godly character, prayer, and evangelism.

The following categories may help you begin to think through potential topics you could cover with your disciple. These categories are in no particular order, and you can freely jump from one to the other. However, make sure she thoroughly understands each topic in the "Basic Walk with God" category before moving on to the others, as those lessons are foundational.

Basic Walk with God

Assurance of salvation

Experience of forgiveness

Spirit-filled life

Identity in Christ

Local church and fellowship

Regular time with God

Sharing the gospel

Developing Godly Character

Teachability

Holiness

Submission to authority

Conflict resolution

Personal purity

Humility

Forgiving attitude

The Bible

Final authority

Study of Scripture

Memorization

Reliability of the Scriptures

Prayer

Commitment to prayer

Spiritual warfare

Praise and adoration

Praying through Scripture

Hindrances to prayer

Praying according to His will

Evangelism

Heart for the lost

How to share the gospel

Handling difficult questions

Definition of successful witnessing

Sharing your personal testimony

Basic apologetics

Different worldviews, religions, cults

Making Disciples

Eternal perspective

Leading a Bible study

Discipleship appointments

Discipling cross-culturally

Speaking the truth in love

Selecting disciples

Commitment sheet

Evangelism in discipleship

"World Christian" mindset

Developing a heart for the world

Great Commission

Praying for the world

Lordship of time, talent, resources

Partaking in mission trips

Giving for world evangelization

Leadership

Correct motivation

Approachability

Humility

Receiving criticism

Communicating clear vision

Developing people, not using them

Delegation

Understanding one's strengths and weaknesses

A Few Suggestions

If the woman is a new believer, I suggest beginning with the category "Basic Walk with God." If she's been a Christian for some time, you might want to show her this list of topics and ask her to pinpoint her weakest areas.

Also, you will find that "Sharing the gospel" is in the first category. Don't make the mistake of not talking about this early in your relationship with your new disciple. We are Christ's ambassadors, and sharing our faith is a basic element in our relationship with God. The disciple doesn't have to be "ready" or have learned extensively in order to talk to others about Christ.

These categories are certainly not exhaustive; there are plenty of other topics you could teach. For example, I have lessons prepared on jealousy, creating good boundaries, and learning to hear God's voice. Once you choose a topic, you'll need to prepare a small lesson to teach the content to your disciple.

The Word

Reading and studying a book of the Bible chapter by chapter is another excellent way for you and your disciple to grow in your walks with God. I usually start with the Book of James. It takes about five to six weeks to read and discuss, and is filled with tons of things easily applicable to one's life. For a simple way to study a book of the Bible, please see www.lorijoiner.com.

Units

Personally, I tend to think in units. I like to choose a topic and spend three to four weeks teaching it, discussing it, and applying it to our lives. Over time I've developed teaching units on such topics as spiritual warfare, writing a life mission statement, sexual purity, and inductive Bible study methods. Jennifer, a woman I discipled, wrote a four-week unit on the parables of Jesus. Each time she met with her disciples, they read and discussed a different parable.

Books and Workbooks

These can be another great source of material. Bridget (a woman I discipled) and I read through This Was Your Life by Rick Howard and Jamie Lash. We read a chapter each week and discussed what we'd learned at appointments. Some other good books and resources are:

Spiritual Disciplines by Richard Foster

Bondage Breakers by Neil Anderson

Breaking Free, When Godly People do Ungodly Things and other Beth Moore books and workbooks

The Case for Christ and *The Case for Faith* by Lee Strobel (also good to read with those investigating Christianity)

Discipleship Journal magazine, which has tons of pre-made lessons on great topics that I've used throughout the years (if you don't already subscribe, I'd encourage you to do so)

Life Concepts, basic foundational lessons primarily used with new believers (order online at www.campuscrusade.com)

On occasion, my disciple and I will go to a Christian bookstore together and pick out a workbook on a topic we both think would be interesting to study. So feel free to include them in the process.

CDs

The following two CDs are loaded with great pre-made lessons, teacher's notes, and articles you can print and use during your discipleship time.

The Compass is designed to help disciplers guide others through the process of becoming mature disciples. In addition to over 45 lesson files, The Compass contains a number of other resources including a series of four talks on the right reasons, people, components, and content for discipleship.

Cru. Comm is a small group Bible study curriculum designed with a logical progression, that in the course of 3-4 years, could take a new Christian, ground them in the basics of the faith and grow them into a Christ-centered laborer.

Both can be ordered online at www.campuscrusade.com.

How to Prepare a Lesson from Scratch

Pre-made Bible studies on CDs or in Christian bookstores can be very helpful. There might be occasions, however, when you want to teach a certain topic for which you will not be able to find a pre-written Bible study. Furthermore, at some point, a good step will be to write your own lessons. This doesn't have to be extremely lengthy or time-consuming. I've written many little "nuggets" from the Bible, and they've been very helpful as I seek to open the Word together with the women I disciple. Below is a basic outline for writing and preparing your own "nuggets" from the Word.

1. Begin with a Scripture passage or verse.

This could be a verse you've studied or come across in your own time studying the Word. Maybe you heard it in a recent sermon, or perhaps memorized it while going through a difficult time.

2. Do your homework.

Research the passage by reading commentaries, study Bibles, or online resources for insight and background into the passage. This important step ensures that you teach the passage correctly and in context. You don't want to infuse your opinion into the verses.

3. Get personal.

Think of a specific example from your own life that goes along with this passage or verse. You want your example to be candid and transparent. Also, brainstorm a few questions that will get your disciple thinking about how this passage or verse applies to her own life.

Below are three examples of "nuggets" I wrote a few years ago that I still pull out of my files and use with the women I disciple. Feel free to use them yourself, or look to them as a guide, when you write your own "nuggets".

Some Examples of a "Nugget" From the Word

NUGGET | JAMES 3:1-12

Begin by sharing your personal example:

I did a humbling thing today. I had spoken ill about a friend of mine and needed to tell her I was sorry. It was difficult; I asked her to forgive me, and she did. I just wish my mouth did not get me into so much difficulty and pain sometimes...

Then read James 3:1-12 and share additional insights you found as you researched it.

Second, ask a few of the questions you brainstormed for discussion:

Do you ever struggle with trying to control what you say?

Do you have a recent example you would like to share?

What is the tongue compared to in this passage?

NUGGET | PSALM 139:13-16

Begin by sharing your personal example:

Lately I seem to compare myself often with other girls in my classes, sorority, etc. It seems like everywhere I look, I somehow fall short. Some of my friends can eat and eat, and their metabolism is so high they don't gain an inch. Not to mention, I hate my hair…

Then read Psalm 139:13-16 and share additional insights you found as you researched it.

Second, ask a few of the questions you brainstormed for discussion:

What do you think it means to have a healthy self-image?

How would you put the truths of this passage into your own words?

How easy is it to accept these truths about yourself? What obstacles keep you from fully accepting them?

NUGGET | PSALM 32

Begin by sharing your personal example:

Sometimes when I sin, I feel like I don't know what to do. I have messed up so many times in this area (maybe name a particular habit you are trying to break, such as lust, criticism, gossip, etc.). I feel like if I go to God again, He won't believe me when I tell him I am really sorry this time.

Then read Psalm 32 and share additional insights you found as you re-searched it.

Second, ask a few of the questions you brainstormed for discussion:

What stands out to you the most from the passage?

According to this psalm, what are some of the benefits of being honest with God about our sin?

According to David, what are the consequences when we're not honest with God about sin?

In Summary

Finding the right material to use with your disciple doesn't have to be difficult or stressful. First, find out where they are at spiritually, and then decide what would be the best next step. Always start with the basics of walking with God, as this will create a solid foundation upon which she can continue to build. By utilizing the Bible, other books and workbooks, and CDs, you'll have plenty of topics and lessons. I've found that preparing a lesson to use in discipleship always helps me learn that topic in a deeper way. There've been countless times when I pause to thank the Lord, praise Him, and confess sin as I prepare a lesson for a discipleship appointment.

 **PART II**

Issues Women Face

Introduction

Because of the nature of discipleship relationships, we will often have a deep connection with the women we disciple. As we pray for them, encourage them, and hope for them, we will develop an ever-deepening desire to see them become all they can be in God's kingdom. So when your disciple shares with you a deep issue in her life, I want you to be equipped to know the next step to take — to know how to respond, how to help, how to point her in the right direction for healing, and how to continue to walk alongside her as her discipler, cheerleader, and friend.

When your disciple reveals a deep issue such as depression, sexual abuse, or a past abortion, you may feel inadequate to deal with such issues. I understand, as I have been there countless times throughout the years. I remember several occasions where I would meet with a woman who confided in me about a particular issue or struggle, and I would immediately pray in my heart, "Oh, God, help me — give me your wisdom. I need your help ASAP."

These next few chapters are written for just those moments. In those situations, you may find yourself with no idea what to say or do next. As you read each chapter, please keep a few things in mind.

First, it is okay not to have the answers. No one, no matter how long they have been discipling others, is equipped in very circumstance. So let yourself off the hook. You are not Superwoman, and it is perfectly fine to say, "I don't know, but I want to help."

Second, you and I are not professional counselors. Okay, maybe a few of those reading this book are professionals, but the majority of us are not. I say this because I don't want you to try to be a counselor in someone else's life. When an issue arises, you need to continue to be the discipler. That is, you can pray together, do outreach together, hang out together, have accountability, and you can teach your disciple from the Bible. But be quick to let someone else do the work of professional counselors. They are trained to understand and find root issues behind certain types of behaviors and ways of thinking, and they will know if the woman you are discipling needs medication, group therapy, or counseling.

Third, the stories in these chapters are real (as throughout the entire book). I want you to have hope for your disciple. Regardless of the problem she is dealing with, she can come through it in the power of the Holy Spirit, and even begin to help others with similar issues. So take heart and don't be discouraged — nothing is impossible with God!

Finally, I want to let you know I am proud of you! Discipling women is a passion and a very rewarding blessing. It can also be a thankless, draining, and heartbreaking endeavor. I have experienced the gamut of emotions, and I am proud of you for persevering and trusting God to work in and through you to touch the lives of others for His glory!

The American Association of Christian Counselors has an entire website dedicated to helping you find in your area the Christian counseling your disciple needs. So if you are discipling a woman you think needs a counselor, have her visit www.aacc.net, click Find a Counselor, and simply enter her zip code. She will then be given a list of counselors in her area whom she could contact to start getting the help she needs.

 **ISSUE #1**

Daughters and Their Fathers: "Can I really trust You, Lord?"

Madison had a difficult relationship with her father. When she was a little girl, her parents divorced. Every other weekend her dad would come to their house and pick up her and her two older brothers. Her dad would then promptly drop her off at her grandmother's house and spend the rest of the weekend with her brothers fishing and hunting. All the while she would be at her grandmother's house.

The neglect of his role as her dad is obvious now, but at the time Madison could not understand why her father spent time with her brothers but not her. The hurt was deep. Her father also had a punishing type of personality, and if she did something he didn't like, he would punish her by shaming her, withholding from her emotionally and financially, and not looking her in the eye when speaking to her. This reinforced the fact that she felt invisible to him.

When it came to Madison's relationship with her heavenly Father, she saw Him as punishing as well. When she would sin, she would wonder, "What is God going to withhold from me?" She wanted to trust God for things in her life, but years of being neglected by her father made her wonder, "Can I really trust you, Lord? I'm just not sure…"

On the Other Hand

"Lori, I am so proud of you," my dad said after my college graduation ceremony.

These words were very familiar to me. He had said them to me all throughout my life. Whether it was a high school play, a talent show or a swim meet, my dad was there cheering me on, affirming his love for me, and telling me he was proud of me. I remember one day when we were sitting on the couch watching TV when the news came on, and he said, "Lori, you could do that. You could do that better than them." He was referring to the news anchors. With a background in speech and theater, he never doubted that I could be and do anything I wanted to, even being a news anchor. I am fortunate to have a dad that loves me, teaches me things, and prays for me.

At the age of 16, when I put my faith in Christ and began to build a personal relationship with God, I began to tell God I wanted Him to be proud of me. I wonder where I got that from? I did not understand at the time how my dad's influence on me, his love for me, and his pride in me helped tremendously when I was beginning to fall in love with God.

I saw God as loving, affectionate, and proud of me. I trusted God to help me, nurture and care for me.

In telling my story, I don't want to paint the wrong picture. I did not grow up in a perfect family. My parents are divorced, and I have lived through some awful situations. However, I never doubted my dad or my mom's love for me. They told me they loved me all the time, they hugged and kissed me, and even when I would really mess up, I knew they loved me and would cheer me on in life.

Many women do not have the same fond memories of their own fathers. Some have been neglected by their fathers, some have been emotionally or sexually abused, and others have been abandoned by their dads all together. How a woman relates to her father can have a huge impact on how she will view God. Identifying the lies your disciple believes about God because of a broken relationship with her father will directly affect how she grows and develops in her relationship with her heavenly Father. If a woman had a loving, nurturing father, then her view of God will often be positive. She will most likely feel that she can trust God, that He loves her, and that He is in her corner looking out for her best interest. On the other hand, if a woman has a neglectful, distant, absent, or even abusive father, her relationship with God could be negatively affected. She will be more prone to have an unhealthy fear of God, have trouble trusting Him, and feel as if He doesn't care about her life or her well-being.

Red Flags

If your disciple displays some of the characteristics listed below, she might have an issue in this area. Realize that if she does have a distorted view of God, she might not even know it. She just sees God that way because of a hurtful relationship with her father, and it is probably not something she consciously chooses to do. However, if you consistently see or hear these things in your disciple's life, a distorted view of God may be hindering her walk with God:

* Does not trust God to provide for her

* Views God as punishing, shrinking back from Him instead of confessing sin

* Feels like she is on her own with no one to lean on

* Has difficulty telling God she loves or adores Him, or using any other affectionate term

* Has been emotionally or sexually abused by her father or other male authority figure

* Has been neglected by her father

* Has not been supported financially or emotionally by her father

* Felt as if her father had "favorites"

* Felt her father compared her with her other siblings or other people in general

* Felt her father was not appropriately affectionate with her by giving her hugs, kisses, and pats on the back

* Did not hear her father tell her that he loved her without any conditions, that she was precious, that she was valuable

* Has constant problems with men in her life (seeking attention, settling for men who are hurtful or not good for her just to fill that void in her life)

If you pick up on these areas as you spend time with your disciple, begin to pray and look for an opportunity to address your observations with her.

The Process of Healing

When it comes to our heavenly Father, we need to strive to see Him the way He desires us to see Him as outlined in the Bible. By understanding the truth of how God our Father views us, we can have the abundant relationship with God He desires for us to have. If you discern that your disciple may have some difficulties in this area, then read and work through these six items:

1. Pray that God would heal wounded areas in your life and help you see Him for the loving, caring father He is.

2. Research what the Bible says about God, His character, and His love for you.

3. Examine your beliefs about God that are inconsistent with what the Bible says.

4. Identify where the devil has sown seeds of lies and mistrust.

5. Confess and repent for wrong beliefs you have about God.

6. Forgive people who have hurt you.

Please understand that I am not trying to minimize the years of stinging pain by giving a six-step outline to remedy a broken relationship. I realize that monstrous situations have sometimes taken place, and neglect, hurtful words, and hurtful actions have caused tremendous pain. I do, though, desire to give hope. The six steps listed above are a place to begin to walk out of pain and replace distortions about God with His truth in Scripture. You can help your disciple begin to release bitterness and forgive those who have caused so much hurt.

Listen First

When you meet with your disciple and begin to talk about this area in her life, be careful not to minimize years of hurt by pushing through too quickly to a solution. Tell her you see the pain in her life and want to help her through it. Validate what she has gone through by listening, asking good questions, and grieving with her. For as long as it takes, let her fully share the pain, emotional scars, and shattered dreams.

At some point, you can begin to turn the corner and say something such as, "I can't imagine what you have gone through in life. I am amazed you have carried this for as long as you have. Do you think the hardships you have had with your father have had any effect on your relationship with God or how you see God?" Again, you are letting her talk and grieve, so continue to actively listen and ask good questions.

You could then respond by saying, "I care for you so much and want to help you and walk through this with you. You are special to God, and He loves you very much. I would love to take as much time as needed over the next few weeks and months to help you see that for yourself."

Walking Through This For the First Time

If you have never done this before or need a bit of a refresher, here is a sample of what this time with your disciple might look like:

1. Pray that God would heal wounded areas in her life and help her see Him for the loving, caring Father He is.

You could ask, "Could we just take some time to pray? God loves you and desires you to trust Him fully and see Him the way He really is. Let's ask Him for help in this process." Remember that this is a long process. It won't all happen in one time together. In His grace, God does not reveal the painful memories to us all at once.

2. Research what the Bible says about God, His character, and His love for you.

Here you could ask, "Why don't we spend some time today just reading and browsing through God's Word looking for verses that describe His nature, His fatherhood, and His love for you." Here are a few of my favorites:

Proverbs 17:19: "The Lord is righteous in all his ways and loving towards all he has made" (NIV).

Romans 5:8: "God demonstrates his own love toward us, in that while we were still sinners, Christ died for us" (NIV).

Psalm 27:10: "Though my father and mother forsake me, the Lord will receive me" (NIV).

Psalm 34:18: "The Lord is close to the brokenhearted, and saves those who are crushed in spirit" (NIV).

Psalm 61:4: "I long to dwell in your tent forever and take refuge in the shelter of your wings" (NIV).

Zephaniah 3:17: "The Lord your God is with you; he is mighty to save. He will take great delight in you, he will quiet you with his love, he will rejoice over you with singing" (NIV).

3. Examine beliefs about God that are inconsistent with what the Bible says.

Suzanne wept bitterly with me one afternoon. She told me about her father, whom she seldom saw and who never called her. When she took the initiative and called him, he always seemed to be in a hurry. To add to this pain, her dad had remarried and had two other children. Sadly, her father provided for these two children financially, went to their softball games, and was actively involved in their lives but not hers. She was understandably very hurt and angry. She longed to be loved and cared for the same way.

Suzanne was a Christian, but her relationship with her father had negatively affected her relationship with her heavenly Father. She felt like she could not trust God, and that He was distant and did not really care for her.

So at this step, you could ask, "Based on what we have read in Scripture, do you think God relates to you the way your father does?"

After we talked at length, she was able to pinpoint what she wrongly believed about God because of her father. She had a distorted view of God, believing this lie: "God does not care about me, God does not help me, and God has his favorites."

4. Identify where Satan has sown seeds of lies and mistrust.

Satan wants to take things that have hurt us in life and use them to get us to turn away from God. He will sow lies into our hearts about God, using our hardships in life as his ammunition.

Just ask her plainly, "Where do you think Satan has purposefully used the difficult things that have happened in your life to turn you away from God, or to mistrust His character?"

5. Confess and repent for wrong beliefs about God.

Pray with your disciple about how the lies of Satan and the wrongdoings of others cloud the truth about God and His love and goodness. Here is a prayer you might consider showing her as a means of helping her express what is on her heart:

"Father, I repent of not believing the truth about you. I am so hurt by not having a dad like I thought I should have had. My heart yearns to have a father that I can lean on, count on, and who will take care of me. I recognize that you are that loving heavenly Father to me. I can count on You and trust in You, and I believe you love me and have the best in store for me. Please help me replace lies with biblical truth."

Encourage your disciple to continue replacing habitual wrong thoughts with truth from Scripture.

6. Forgive people who have inflicted pain.

This step is crucial. We, as well as the women we are discipling, need to forgive our father (or mother or anybody who has hurt us). If we hang onto bitterness and unforgiveness, we will short-circuit the abundant life God wants us to have. Bitterness hurts the person who holds it more than the person it is intended for. Just think: your father probably doesn't even realize the pain you have gone through. He probably would not know how to apologize adequately if he did. We hurt ourselves by not forgiving him. Ask the Lord to help your disciple walk in forgiveness just as the Lord has forgiven her.

A Few Extras

Take Your Time

Going through these steps with your disciple will be important as she reads about God from His Word, uncovers lies of Satan, and forgives people who have wronged or hurt her. Don't rush this process. These steps could take anywhere from one appointment to a five-week unit where you take each step week by week. So take your time, because making sure your disciple has a correct view of God is paramount to her growth and ever-deepening relationship with God.

Pray Again and Again

Continue to pray for your disciple daily. You might be the only one praying for her in this area. Send her encouraging messages about God as well as verses that point to His love for her, His character, and His provision for her. During your discipleship appointments and other times you spend together, listen for thoughts she might share that are inconsistent with God's Word, and then lovingly point her back to who God really is as revealed in Scripture.

Two Mathematical Equations

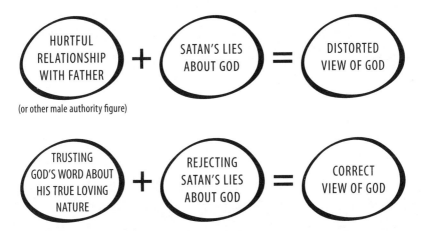

(or other male authority figure)

In very simple terms, there are two equations we can constantly reaffirm in our lives. One will continually equal a distorted view of God, and the other will consistently equal a correct view of God. As a loving discipler, help your disciple begin to learn about God's true loving nature and to avoid comparing Him to the hurtful situations she has encountered with her own father figure.

Books for Additional Help

Who I Am in Christ, Neil Anderson

The Father Heart of God, Floyd McClung

God: Discover His Character, Bill Bright

The Cry for Spiritual Fathers and Mothers, Larry Kreider

Forgive and Live, Beth Hunter

Making Peace with Your Father, David Stoop, Ph.D.

Father Hunger, Robert S. McGee

The Search for Significance, Robert S. McGee

In Summary

Distorted views of God are sometimes the result of difficult or non-existent relationships women have with their earthly fathers, a lack of time in the Word, and believing Satan's lies about God and self. Identifying these lies in your life and then helping your disciple identify them in hers will help you both grow closer to the Lord and see Him as He truly is — our loving, providing, patient Heavenly Father — and see ourselves as a child of God who is worthy, significant, forgiven, and deeply loved.

 **ISSUE #2**

Eating Disorders: "If I eat this, it will make me fat…"

"I remember the first day I threw up," Allison told me. "I was on a Girl Scout camping trip and felt I had eaten too much. Just that week I had watched a Baywatch episode where the star of the show, played by Pamela Anderson, was being confronted with her eating disorder. There was a detailed scene showing her character throwing up her food by sticking her fingers down her throat. So I excused myself to the bathroom and tried to do what I had just seen on television — throw up by putting my fingers down my throat. It worked, and so began my six-year battle with bulimia.

"In high school, I began to date Justin. 'Awful' is the only way to describe him accurately. He wanted me to be super-skinny and encouraged me to do anything to stay thin, even if it meant throwing up my food. He would say things like, 'You are so beautiful and skinny.' Struggling with low self-esteem, I did my best to please him and stay thin by continually throwing up my food. It became more than just something I did every once in a while; I was now bingeing and purging three or four times a day."

Upon returning from a date, Allison would grab an entire box of Raisin Bran and milk. "Any food taken with milk or Coke would always make the throwing-up part a lot easier," Allison continued. "I would binge on Raisin Bran, milk, and Coke, and then purge it after every date I went on. I just couldn't cope with how he treated me. I felt used and worthless, and bingeing was my solace. Each morning when I woke up, I hated myself. I hated myself for throwing up, I hated that I did not feel like I could stop bingeing, and I hated having a boyfriend who only liked me if I was skinny. And to make matters worse, any food I was tempted to eat, I thought to myself, 'If I eat this, it will make me fat.'"

Allison had become accustomed to her dry mouth, aching throat, and what she calls "chipmunk cheeks." "My face and cheeks were so swollen from the trauma of throwing up all day that it literally looked like I had something stuck in my cheeks," she said. "Even now, I cannot look at pictures from those years. It's just too painful."

When Allison's hair began falling out in chunks, she realized the extent of her addiction. She approached her mom with the news of her problem, and her mom responded simply, "Just don't do that." Allison was reaching out for help, but still felt stuck. No longer trying to hide her secret, she would walk into a bathroom, even with three other girls in the next room, and purge her entire dinner.

There are many reasons women struggle with eating disorders, including a need for control, a distorted body image, media propaganda and fear. Eating disorders are complex. The roots of these issues often have nothing to do with food at all. If someone you disciple has an eating disorder, this chapter will help you understand the warning signs, the different types of disorders, and how to walk through the healing process.

Referring to a Professional Counselor

The rest of this chapter will give you helpful information I have compiled about this issue through the years. Be assured that 99.9 percent of us are not equipped to fully help a woman with a history of eating disorders. At any moment feel free to say to her, "I really want to help you and I don't have the resources you need. I think you need to see someone who specializes in this area, so I would love to help connect you with a professional counselor and continue to walk through this with you."

So as you read, take note of information and testimonies you think could help your disciple, but don't feel pressured to become her counselor. Just continue to pray for her, spend time with her, help her grow spiritually, and encourage her to be an overcomer.

Red Flags

There are numerous types of eating disorders: compulsive overeating, exercise addiction, anorexia, bulimia, and any mix of these together. Here I will cover some of the warning signs for three of the more common eating disorders.

Anorexia nervosa is essentially self-starvation. An anorexic will do her best to go long periods of time without eating. This disorder is characterized by:

* ❋ Preoccupation with food, calories, nutrition, and cooking

* Denial of hunger

* Excessive exercise

* Frequent weighing

* Loss of menstrual cycle

* Claiming to feel "fat" when in reality she isn't

* Dieting with zeal when not overweight

* Odd combinations of food

* Intermittent episodes of "binge" eating

Bulimia nervosa means eating or overeating (bingeing), then throwing up (purging) afterward. Symptoms include:

* Excessive concern about weight

* Strict dieting followed by eating binges

* Frequent overeating, especially when distressed

* Expressing guilt or shame about eating, feeling out of control, depressive moods

* Use of laxatives and/or vomiting to control weight

* Leaving for the bathroom after meals (secretive vomiting)

* Planning binges or opportunities to binge

* Fear of eating in front of people

Binge-eating disorder (compulsive overeating) is eating when not hungry, or continual eating without regard to physiological cues. It is often mistakenly considered to be less serious than

other disorders and therefore often undiagnosed. Here are some symptoms:

* ❋ Frequently eating to the point of extreme discomfort and pain

* ❋ Bingeing to reduce anxiety or deal with emotional problems

* ❋ Preoccupation with body image

* ❋ Eating in secret, such as in the car or in the middle of the night

* ❋ Inability to stop or control eating once a binge ritual has begun

* ❋ Compulsive behaviors, inflexibility, and excess in life in general

* ❋ Total preoccupation with food

Note: Not all people with binge-eating disorder are overweight, and not all overeaters are binge eaters.

Bringing Up the Subject

Your disciple may tell you she is struggling in this area and needs help. Or you may need to initiate the conversation yourself after seeing some of the aforementioned red flags. I can say without a doubt that this is one of the hardest things for me to do. I always have to overcome fear that I might offend the person when my heart is to help them. Here is a personal experience of how I brought this subject up with Tina, a woman I was discipling.

A few years ago, I began to suspect that Tina was struggling with an eating disorder. I noticed that in social eating scenes, she would put a ton of food on her plate, only to eat a few bites, excuse herself, and dump the plate of food down the sink and say, "I'm full." In one instance I became aware that she had only eaten a can of tuna and dry lettuce all day. She was already very thin and had low self-esteem. She walked and exercised constantly.

I did not know what to do. I was afraid to bring it up, thinking that if I was wrong, I would really offend her. Time after time, though, she would not eat, and she was becoming dangerously thin. I prayed fervently that God would help me initiate the conversation, that He would prepare her heart to talk about this, and that ultimately He would heal her and set her free.

"Tina," I said during our regular discipleship time one afternoon, "I don't really know how to bring this up. I don't want to hurt you. But because I care for you, I am going to bring this up, and trust God with the outcome. I have noticed that some of your eating behaviors don't seem normal." I then explained to her the observations I had made, and then said, "Are you having some trouble in this area? Are your eating patterns as bizarre as I have noticed? Or is what I am saying coming out of left field?"

Tina's eyes began to well up with tears. She nodded her head yes, and there began a long process of healing from her addiction to this disorder. As with most eating disorders, Tina had some family dynamic issues that manifested in her strict control of food. When Tina was growing up, she was not allowed to be herself. She was not allowed to express herself or allow her own personality to develop. For example, her mom made her wear very frilly dresses, style her hair a certain way, and even enter beauty pageants. It was as if Tina's mom was living her life through Tina. She exerted a severe control over who Tina was, prohibiting Tina from being herself.

Knowing Tina now, I can't imagine her in beauty pageants or wearing frilly dresses. She is very natural, wears little makeup, and loves to shop at hip thrift stores. Tina is beautiful and soft-spoken, and hates to be in front of people. One way she found she could express herself was through food and how much she did or did not eat. This was one area in her life that Tina could control. And this habit she had formed to find some semblance of control was now controlling her.

Understanding the Extent

When talking about eating issues with your disciple, one way to fully understand the extent of her problem is to ask a few questions. Here is a list I have compiled and used throughout the years. After you have talked about your concerns, you could introduce this by saying, "I want to understand the extent of what is going on in your life so I can fully grasp your struggle and get you the help you need. In order for me to do that, how would you feel about me asking you a few questions?" Feel free to bring this list with you:

1. Do you have regular periods? Skip periods?

2. Do you fear getting fat?

3. How often do you count calories/fat grams?

4. How often and how long do you exercise?

5. Do you "punishment-eat" (for example, deny yourself dinner because you ate a large lunch, or punish yourself for eating seconds by restricting food at the next meal)?

6. Have you talked with anyone about this before? If yes, what was done?

7. When did this start? How old were you?

8. Why did this start?

9. Have you ever thrown up your food? How often?

10. Do you purposely skip meals when hungry? Go a day without eating? Longer?

11. What do you believe some of the root causes are?

12. What is the longest you have gone without eating?

13. Do you eat in the middle of the night?

14. Do you tend to eat in secret?

As you ask these questions and learn more about the extent, you will be better able to help your disciple. These questions will also help you possibly narrow down the exact type of eating disorder she has. She may be just on the outskirts of an eating disorder, and your relationship with her will provide the love, support, and accountability she needs. If her patterns are deep, long, and life-threatening, she will most likely need to see a professional counselor for more in-depth treatment, as I mentioned before.

Root Issues

Getting at the root of an eating disorder is paramount for complete recovery. Your disciple, in her own strength, may be able to eat normally for a while, but it will only be a matter of time before the unresolved root issue resurfaces again. Listed below are some common root issues in this area, as well as the understanding that your disciple will eventually need to come to for lasting recovery.

Your disciple will need to:

* Understand that her eating disorder is not about food or fat

* Understand that her eating disorder is a coping mechanism to deal with pain

* Heal from trauma, sexual abuse, and other painful experiences in her past

* Face fears of being unacceptable and unloved, and find better ways to deal with those fears than through perfectionism

* Develop a healthy self-esteem and reject self-hatred and self-loathing

* Resolve her issues with food, health, and nutrition so she can live

* Want to live and be alive

* Resolve body-image issues and stop determining self-worth by size and shape

* Give herself permission to feel and eat, and to ask for and receive help

* Trust herself and others, rather than demand to be in control

* Forgive herself

Most of this portion was adapted from information gathered at CenterforChange.com.

Turning Points

Each woman or friend I have known through the years who has struggled with an eating disorder has shared with me her "turning point" — a thought, realization, or Scripture verse that helped her truly begin to seek the Lord for help battling the disorder. I wanted to include them, as you may find one that may be particularly helpful in your disciple's specific situation.

Sin

Referring back to the story that opened this chapter, when Allison was confronted with the fact that bingeing and purging was a sin, she was shocked. She knew it was not something she should be doing, but did not necessarily consider it a sin. Nevertheless, it is. God has given us an "earth-suit," on loan, to be able to do His will and fulfill His purpose for our lives. When we starve ourselves, purge our food, or overeat, we are treating our earth-suits contrary to what they were designed to do. That is sin. Our bodies are temples of the Holy Spirit and should be treated with care. As Romans 12:1 reminds us, "Therefore, I urge you, brothers, in view of God's mercy, to offer your bodies as living sacrifices, holy and pleasing to God—this is your spiritual act of worship" (NIV).

Our bodies are not our own. We are to present them to God in worship, as vessels for Him to use to touch people for His kingdom. When we give Him our bodies, healthy and ready for service unto Him, that is an act of worship: "Do not offer the parts of your body to sin, as instruments of wickedness, but rather offer yourselves to God, as those who have been brought from death to life; and offer the parts of your body to him as instruments of righteousness" (Romans 6:13, NIV).

Allison said that she would talk to God about her bingeing and purging, and even begged God to let her do it because it was the only way she thought she could stay thin. She was scared to trust God with her weight. She felt certain that if she trusted God and stopped throwing up her food, He would make her fat. After years of repeatedly trying to stop, giving in, and feeling guilty, Allison finally took a shaky step of trust and gave it to God: "I told the Lord I would rather be fat and walk with Him than be thin and not walk with Him."

Eternal Perspective

One day, as a friend and I were talking about eating disorders, I casually commented, "It's sad that a woman who has an eating disorder will spend years of her life obsessed with every calorie, hiding a secret sin of bulimia, anorexia, etc., all to shed the body and spend eternity in heaven. It's like all her time went to something that is not eternal, something that won't last past her brief time on earth." My friend later told me that was a huge eye-opener for her regarding her own eating issues. Psalm 39:4-5 reminds us, "Show me, O Lord, my life's end and the number of my days; let me know how fleeting is my life. You have made my days a mere handbreadth; the span of my years is as nothing before you. Each man's life is but a breath" (NIV).

In the grand scheme of things, we don't have a whole lot of time on earth. I once heard it said that if you add up all the days of time, our lives would seem like a mere weekend in comparison. We need to help our disciples invest their "weekend" in something that will last. Their soul, their relationship with God, and the souls of others — these things will last, not our bodies, which will ultimately perish.

Leaning on God

Another turning point for many women is the reminder that they are not alone in the healing process. Remind your disciple that she has God's strength to help her overcome the temptation of bingeing, purging, and starving. The Holy Spirit dwells within us, and we can ask Him for help, guidance, and strength in the face of temptation. As Psalm 46:1 tells us, "God is our refuge and strength, an ever-present help in trouble" (NIV).

As difficult as it may seem to reject the temptation to overeat or binge, God will help us. He will not allow us to be tempted beyond what we are able to endure: "No temptation has seized you except what is common to man. And God is faithful; he will not let you be tempted beyond what you can bear. But when tempted, he will also provide a way out so that you can stand up under it" (1 Corinthians 10:13, NIV).

Bigger Purpose

Remind your disciple of the truth of God's Word: We are His workmanship and we are delightfully made. We have a destiny to fulfill, and our bodies, eyes, voice, and personality have been fashioned by God to help us achieve that. We can trust God with this area of our lives; He is trustworthy and cares for us more that we could ever comprehend: "For we are God's workmanship, created in Christ Jesus to do good works, which God prepared in advance for us to do" (Ephesians 2:10, NIV).

Idolatry

Tina would lie awake at night thinking about her body and weight. She would calculate everything she had eaten that day and determine what had been good and what had been bad. If she had eaten too much at any one meal, that was bad, and she would scold herself. If she had curbed hunger pains by only drinking water, then that was good. Before falling asleep she would mentally go through everything she would allow herself to eat the next day, and she would drift asleep only after she was convinced she had a game plan she could follow.

In the morning, she would shower and spend a long time in front of the mirror. She would look at every square inch of her body, berating herself for areas she felt were intolerably fat. She would then give herself a pep talk regarding what she was and was not going to allow herself to eat that day. She would make deals with herself and impose consequences if she failed to follow through on her extremely low-calorie diet.

All throughout the day, Tina's mind focused on what she had just eaten, whether it had been good or bad, what she was going to eat, how to deal with her constant hunger pains, new ways to get thin, and a constant fear of being fat. All of Tina's attention and energy was focused on herself. She was her own idol.

In the Old Testament, the people of God made and worshipped a golden calf, as well as other man-made objects. They put these idols before God, at times even in the place of God: "You shall not make for yourself an idol in the form of anything in heaven above or earth beneath or in the waters below. You shall not bow down to them or worship them; for I, the Lord your God, am a jealous God..." (Exodus 20:4, NIV).

God forbids us to worship other idols. He is a jealous God and desires, even demands, to hold first place in our lives. An idol is anything we put before God.

Some women put their boyfriends before God. All their time and thoughts are spent on these men. God is pushed to the side, receiving only the leftovers of their emotional energy and time. Some women put their careers before God. Their long hours may make church or time with the Lord a mere afterthought. Other women put entertainment before the Lord. In truth, anything taken out of its healthy function and abused may become an idol, whether it take the form of exercise, shopping, food, or even our very own bodies! We need to be very careful not to make an idol out of anything or anyone.

Tina told me her turning point came not only when she faced her own pain and family issues, but also when she realized the idol she had made of herself. She wanted to focus on her relationship with God and her growing walk with Him, rather than on her own body. She wanted to be a God-worshipper and not a self-worshipper.

A Tale of Two Hearts

As I have discipled women who struggle in this area, I have found two types of hearts. The first is a teachable heart. This woman needs someone to reach out to her, help her, and convince her that she doesn't have to do this to herself. She needs someone to walk through this with her, pray for her, and help her get to the root of her pain. Allison was this type of woman. She had been so hurt by her boyfriend's comments about her body that she needed someone to come alongside her and say, "You're beautiful, and you don't have to be dangerously thin to be beautiful." She wanted help. She wanted to replace the lies with truth, but was unsure where to start.

The other type of woman does not have a teachable heart. You can lovingly share with her your observations about her destructive eating behaviors, and she will flatly deny them. Or she will admit to having an eating disorder, but will not want to change. She may even claim that she is going to change, but in truth has no such intention. In cases such as these, she either wants to continue her established eating habits, which she believes give her control and allows her to be thin, or she is unready to face the painful root issues driving her disorder.

Allison said that she did not have a teachable heart for the first four years of her struggle with bulimia. She had decided that she was going to be thin no matter what, and would not have listened to anybody's advice on the issue. Later, when she realized the extent of her terrible habit, Allison wanted to change. At this point, however, she felt trapped and addicted to the behavior. It was only after all this that her heart slowly became more teachable, and she began to reach out for help.

If you are unsure which type of heart your disciple has, I would encourage you to ask her. Ask if she is ready and willing to begin to heal. You might say to her, "I want to help you with this. I know there are root issues that tend to manifest themselves in eating habits. I am not an expert, but would love to help. Are you willing to trust God with this area of your life and begin to seek Him for help to end this eating disorder?"

Watch Your Language

It is important that we disciplers set a good example in this area by eating normally and expressing a healthy self-image. If I embraced every fad diet, proclaimed certain foods to be "good" or "bad," swore off sweets, and talked non-stop about how "fat" I felt, I believe I could short-circuit my ability to help the women in my life who really do have serious issues with food. They might even think, "If Lori thinks she's fat, I wonder what she thinks about me..."

I ran a ministry home for four years. During that time I had an average of eight girls living with me each year. One of the primary ways I ministered to them was to model a life of exercising regularly, eating normally (three meals a day, plus snacks), and enjoying desserts. A number of these women had struggled with eating issues such as bulimia and compulsive overeating. Observing me accept my body, trust that the Lord designed me uniquely, and eat and exercise regularly helped them perhaps more than any of the Bible studies I ever taught.

All that to say: if you feel like you need to lose weight, do so in a healthy way by eating in moderation and exercising regularly. The only way to truly lose weight and keep it off is through a lifestyle change, not fad diets and quick fixes. Accept your body and reject negative thoughts about yourself that are not coming from God. He loves you. When you are a strong model in this area and can fully accept yourself and embrace a good self-esteem, you will set your disciple up for victory when it comes to eating and food issues.

Helpful Hints

Hold Thoughts Captive

If your disciple is bombarded with negative thoughts, teach her to treat them as lustful or mean thoughts and reject them! They are not from the Lord, and are likely a spiritual attack from Satan. He is a liar who desires us to believe the opposite of what the Lord thinks of us. Satan knows the Lord loves, accepts, and delights in us, and therefore he hurls painful thoughts at us like, "You are fat; God will make you fat; if you eat, you will lose control; being thin is your only hope for happiness."

Does that sound like something God would say? Of course not. Therefore, encourage your disciple to reject such thoughts. We have the ability, and moreover the right, as children of God to replace these lies with

EATING DISORDERS: "IF I EAT THIS, IT WILL MAKE ME FAT..."

scriptural truth. Spend some time with your disciple discussing the thoughts that come into her mind throughout the day related to food, body image, and God. Study God's Word together, looking for Scriptures that combat the negative thoughts. I have included a few to get you started:

> When you begin to think, "If you eat this you will be fat," replace it with "So we fix our eyes not on what is seen, but on what is unseen. For what is seen is temporary, but what is unseen is eternal" (2 Corinthians 4:18, NIV).

> If you find yourself thinking, "You cannot help overeating; it is just who you are," dwell instead on "Therefore, if anyone is in Christ, he is a new creation; the old has gone, the new has come" (2 Corinthians 5:17, NIV).

Accountability

Share your thoughts, emotions, and eating patterns with your disciple and encourage her to talk about hers. Don't be afraid to ask her difficult questions such as, "What did you eat today? Did you get to spend time with God? If not, was it because you worked out instead? Has your body told you it was hungry, and are you denying it?"

If your disciple legitimately needs to lose weight, why not do it together? You can share goals, struggles, and accountability questions to ask each other on a regular basis, to help both of you reach your goals in a healthy way. You can spend time together praying, exercising and cooking meals. As Ecclesiastes 4:9,10 shows us, "Two are better than one, because they have a good return for their work: If one falls down, his friend can help him up. But pity the man who falls and has no one to help him up" (NIV).

Accountability will be extremely helpful when your disciple is tempted to purge her food or not eat despite being legitimately hungry, because she knows you will ask her about it. When she embraces lies instead of believing the truth about herself and her self-worth, you can be there to help her and remind her of her great worth in God.

Limit the Scale

Many women live in bondage to the numbers displayed on their bathroom scale. When a woman steps onto her scale and sees a number that is even a half-pound over what she believes to be acceptable, it can send panic to her mind and cast a shadow on her entire day. I used to do this before I realized that most women will fluctuate a bit in weight during the month and that life was too short to feel bad about half a pound. If you notice that the bathroom scale becomes a hindrance in your disciple's struggle with weight, you might suggest that she consider giving it to a friend and only weigh herself once a week or once a month.

Extra Help for the Binge Eater

Holly lived her entire life by a strict set of rules: "I can only eat pizza on Fridays, I cannot eat fat, if I wake up late I still have to bike and run, I will let myself wear that only if I barely eat today, I will only eat vegetables, I will only, I will only, I will only…" And on it went. Her strict control of food led to episodes of binge eating and incredible feelings of self-hate and guilt. At one point she had restricted her calories so severely that she lost her period for almost a year. "Lord," Holly prayed,

"If you let me have my period back I promise to eat some fat." Struggling with an intense obsession with food, calories, and exercise, Holly's binge eating addiction controlled her for much of her life. She was never told she looked too thin. Most considered Holly to be healthy, self-controlled, and athletic. Sadly, they had no idea of the constant struggle going on inside her mind.

If your disciple is struggling with a binge-eating disorder, she might benefit greatly by meeting with others who share similar problems, since women with this addiction tend to isolate themselves and hide their behaviors. Indeed, any woman with an eating disorder is encouraged to get additional help in the path toward complete healing and victory, whether through books, self-help groups, a Christian counselor, or on-line resources. Also, you might suggest to your disciple who binge-eats in the car to consider taking a different route home, one where she will not be confronted by the temptation of fast-food restaurant chains, or bringing a passenger along for the ride. She should also be encouraged not to bring home unhealthy snacks or "trigger foods."

Aim at the Heart

Remember it's about the heart. Try to aim at the heart and your disciple's continued deepening in her relationship with Jesus. It's not just about behavioral modifications, where she drives, not using the scale, or counting calories. It's about her heart relying on God and yielding to Him in every situation. It's about falling in love with Jesus and facing the struggle in the power of the Holy Spirit, and walking with God day by day, moment by moment.

Additional Help

This chapter only begins to uncover some of the many issues involved with eating disorders. I hope it's given you a place to begin walking with your disciple toward complete victory in this area of her life. If you need additional help, please utilize some of the resources I have included. As I have mentioned before, if your disciple is struggling with an eating disorder, the root often has nothing to do with food at all, and professional help should be sought sooner than later for real help and lasting healing.

Program Information/Contact Information

Remuda Programs, 888-724-0802 or www.remudaranch.com

Eating Disorder Resource Catalogue, 800-756-7533 or www.bulimia.com

Celebrate Recovery Materials and Small Groups, www.celebraterecovery.com

The Lord's Table (Bible study and online accountability for overeaters), www.SettingCaptivesFree.com

Helpful Books

Do You Think I'm Beautiful? Angela Thomas

Loving Your Body, Deborah Newman

Holy Hunger, Margaret Bullitt Jones

Hunger Pains: The Modern Woman's Tragic Quest for Thinness, Mary Pipher, Ph.D.

Diary of an Eating Disorder, Chelsea Browning Smith

Starving for Attention, Cherry Boone O'Nell

Body Betrayed, Kathryn Zarbe, M.D.

When Your Child Has an Eating Disorder: A Step-by-Step Workbook for Parents and Caregivers, Abigail H. Natenshon

In Summary

It has been said that women think about food and their weight as much as men think about sex — meaning we think about it all the time! Many women, due to a variety of factors, have embraced destructive and dangerous eating behaviors to achieve thinness. As disciplers, we can be loving guides in their lives by helping them replace lies about their body with the truth of God's Word, uncover the root of their eating habits, and ultimately gain victory over negative eating patterns.

What is thrilling is that each woman mentioned in this chapter —Allison, Tina, and Holly— have gained healing in this area of life. That does not mean they are perfect. They still report times of intense temptation and consistently have to replace lies with the truth of God's Word. The best part, though, is that each of these women currently disciple other women, helping them walk out of their own eating disorders.

 ISSUE #3

Abortion: "I look in the mirror and think, 'What have I done?'"

"I need to tell you something, and I am not sure how to tell you," Noel said with tears running down her cheeks. "I had an abortion two years ago."

"It was during my sophomore year of college," she continued. "When I saw that pregnancy test turn positive, I was shocked. A million things went through my head at the same time. I said to myself, 'I can't be pregnant, I can't tell my parents, I'm only 19, I'm not even dating the guy anymore, I don't want anyone to know, I don't want it.' I was just over two months pregnant. The father of the baby paid for the abortion, after he told me I had better really be pregnant because he didn't want to waste his money if this was all just a hoax. I wish I could go back and change things. If I knew then what I know now, I would have had that baby and trusted that God would give me an abundant life even as a single parent. I would have had that baby and have raised him even though it would have been really hard. And now every morning I look at myself in the mirror and think, 'What have I done?'"

Many women are grieving the past choice of having an abortion. Whether they were talked into an abortion by someone else (husband, boyfriend, parent, or friend) or had an abortion out of fear, we as disciplers need to be ready to comfort and love women dealing with the aftermath of an abortion.

First Response

After your disciple shares about a past abortion, immediately respond with care, comfort, love, and non-judgmental words and body language. As in any other type of situation where your disciple is hurting because of a past mistake, you need to love her, and tell her you're honored that she shared this with you and glad she felt that she could trust you. Tell her you want to walk through this grief with her the best you can, and that you want be a sounding board and a shoulder to cry on.

The issue here is not to convince her that abortion is wrong. She knows that now. She has told herself that every day since the day she walked out of the abortion clinic. Your role is to love her, reassure her of God's love for her, and remind her that He offers forgiveness. She needs to receive His forgiveness and ask Him for the strength to forgive herself.

Again, in no way do you want to bring up any pro-life propaganda. She has beat herself up more than anyone ever could, so just stay on the path of love, healing, and helping her work through her intense grief. If you have any shred of judgmental thoughts in your heart, please read one of the books listed in the Additional Help section at the end of this chapter to help you have compassion and love for women who have gone through this traumatic event.

In Over Your Head

At this point you may feel a bit in over your head. Your disciple has just shared a very traumatic event in her life, and you may be the first person she has told since the event took place. You are not going to be able to help her through this alone. She needs professional counsel. I would recommend you connect her with a Christian counselor who is better equipped in this area. You can continue to walk beside her in this healing journey as a loving, caring friend. If you try to be the one and only person in her life to help her through this, you may end up harming the healing process in her life, as you most likely don't have the experience or education necessary to really help. I don't either! The rest of this chapter is extra information for your benefit, but is not meant to make a diagnosis or take the place of professional counseling.

Understanding Post-Traumatic Stress Disorder and Post-Abortion Syndrome

Post-Abortion Syndrome, or PAS, is a psychological dysfunction resulting from a traumatic experience (i.e. abortion) that overwhelms a person's normal defense mechanisms, resulting in intense fear, feelings of helplessness, being trapped, or loss of control.

The symptoms of PAS may be delayed for several years, as one of the coping mechanisms a woman uses to deal with her abortion is to suppress the memory of the traumatic event. Some are in denial that it even happened. Usually three to five years after the abortion, a woman will begin to show signs of PAS.

There are three major symptoms of PAS. The first is hyperarousal, characterized by a consistently and inappropriately aroused "fight or flight" defense mechanism. This means that the woman seems to be on a permanent alert for threats of danger. Exaggerated startle responses, anxiety attacks, and outbursts of rage or anger all point to hyperarousal.

Another symptom is intrusion, which is the re-experience of the traumatic event at unwanted and unexpected times. Symptoms of intrusion include recurrent and intrusive thoughts about the abortion or aborted child, nightmares about the abortion or child, or reactions of intense grief or depression on the due date of the aborted pregnancy or the anniversary date of the abortion.

The third symptom of PAS is constriction. This refers to the numbing of emotional resources. It is avoidance behavior — an attempt to deny and avoid people or places that aggravate the negative feelings associated with the abortion. In PAS cases, constriction may include an inability to recall the abortion experience, avoidance of children, withdrawal from those involved in the abortion decision, restricted range of loving or tender feelings, diminished interest in previously enjoyed activities, drug or alcohol abuse, suicidal thoughts or acts, and other self-destructive tendencies.

If you feel your disciple is showing these signs, but has not told you about her abortion, be gentle with her. Affirm to her that you want to help her and walk through hard things with her and that she can tell you anything she has gone through without fear of being judged or condemned. If she won't tell you herself, you need to patiently and lovingly wait until she does. You should recommend she see a counselor who can help her diagnose the root of these symptoms, which may or may not be abortion. If you force a person to tell you what has happened in their life, they will likely run from you.

Most of this information about PAS was adapted from material prepared by The Elliot Institute, one of the nation's leading authorities on post-abortion issues.

Connect Her With Others

Putting her in touch with other women who have had an abortion is pivotal to her healing.

A good friend of mine who was in ministry for years and who holds a master's degree in Christian education gave me advice on this issue. She had an abortion when she was 19 years old and has since experienced a tremendous amount of healing.

"The main goal is to get them to be with other women who've also had abortions and have experienced what they've experienced," she counseled. "There are so many psychological issues involved that unless you've had an abortion you won't be able to really help them. They need to get connected with other women who've had abortions and who can talk with them about all the things they are thinking, experiencing, and going through."

She also added, "Probably the most important thing you could say to a woman who is just beginning to feel the magnitude of what she's done is to tell her to breathe, that she is going to be okay, and that she will make it through this immense, suffocating grief."

To help your disciple get connected to other Christian women who have had abortions, ask leaders at your church if they offer any type of abortion recovery programs. You can also go online to find similar programs or to find someone in your area to speak with in person.

Watch Your Language

As disciplers, we need to be sensitive in our casual talk about abortion, the phrases we use, bumper stickers we put on our cars, etc. We need to be careful not to hinder our disciple from seeking our help and sharing her past mistakes with us. She might not self-disclose about a past abortion if she feels she'll be instantly judged. For example, what do you think the odds are of a woman sharing with her discipler the intense grief she is feeling over her abortion if the discipler has a bumper sticker on her car that says "Abortion is Murder!" Or, said another way, do you think your sister in Christ who is dealing with the shame and pain of an abortion can ask you for prayer if she overheard you say in casual conversation, "Well, at least the girl didn't have an abortion!"?

I am fortunate to have Christian friends who are brutally honest with me. One friend who had an abortion told me how some of my language in the past, while true, was so cutting and hurtful that it drove her away from me instead of to me. That grieved my heart. Instead of helping my friend, I was adding to her hurt with my offhand comments.

So regardless of the issue, whether it's abortion, homosexuality, or something else, be careful not to hurt people in the process of touting your opinions. You never know what the person sitting right next to you has been through and may be grieving over. As disciplers, and Christians for that matter, we need to be safe people filled with grace and compassion, not people filled with angry, hurtful, judgmental words and actions. We need to offer the real peace found in Jesus Christ. We need to continually point people to Him, especially women who are grieving a past abortion.

Additional Help

There is a tremendous amount of helpful resources available to help you and your disciple further with this issue. Here are just a few of the many I found:

SafeHaven Ministries: According to its promotional material, "Safe-Haven is a safe place for those who have had abortions to find comfort, hope, understanding, and healing in the painful aftermath of abortion. We are a peer support site, meaning that most of those who use this site have had an abortion or have been hurt by abortion. As such, we do not judge nor condemn those who have chosen abortion. On the contrary, you will be fully accepted. We are here to help." For more information, visit www.safehavenministries.com.

PATH, Post Abortion Treatment and Healing: www.healingafterabortion.org (fostering compassionate healing and restoration for women wounded by abortion). Counselors available at 407-717-5557.

A Season to Heal: Help and Hope for Those Working Through Post-Abortion Stress, Luci Freed and Penny Salazar

A Solitary Sorrow: Finding Healing and Wholeness After Abortion, Terri Reisser

In Summary

The number of women grieving a past abortion is staggering. It's only a matter of time before you disciple a woman who has had an abortion and at some point will need to begin the healing process. Responding with grace, love, and help is paramount to your disciple being able to talk with you about her grief and experience real healing in her heart. By understanding Post-Abortion Syndrome, you will be able to learn and identify the patterns associated with PAS in the women you are discipling and be able to point them to a Christian counselor and other helpful resources. Also, it is imperative that as disciplers we watch our language, comments, etc., so the women we are discipling can share with us their pain without the fear of rejection and condemnation.

 ISSUE #4

Lesbianism: "Have I crossed a line yet?"

"I was a dancer on tour with a Christian dance troupe," Jamie said. "I loved the stage, the audience, and the thrill of dancing. We traveled all over Europe sharing the message of God's love in cold, communist Russia. I was 16, and dancing was a huge focal point of my life.

"On the road I became very close with Michelle. She was about five years older and had many maternal aspects to her personality. We were constantly together. When I was in junior high I had several crushes on girls, as I simply found them fascinating, and with Michelle I felt the same fascination; I wanted to be with her. I was also confused in my relationship with Michelle, as there seemed to be such a fine line between fun girlfriends and lovers. Each step along the way I would wonder, 'Have I crossed a line yet?'

"The relationship eventually did cross a line and became a lesbian relationship. Another woman on the dance troupe, who had discerned what was going on, confronted Michelle about the relationship with me, and it stopped. It was like scales fell from my eyes, and I knew that this was not a path I wanted to go down in my life. Unfortunately, I also had the feeling this issue was going to come back around.

"Years later, after several serious boyfriends with whom I was sexually involved, I met Rachel. She was from another country and was intelligent and creative. She was older than I was and was screamingly funny. We stayed in touch through letters and phone calls and then she came to visit me and my family in the States. She stayed at my parents' house and even got a part-time job. I was heading down the same path as before and after eight weeks, the relationship got physical one night.

"I was brought up in a Christian home where the truths of God's Word were taught. And so I remember wrestling with God in my heart. I knew it was wrong being in the relationship with Rachel, but I begged Him to let me have it anyway. I would say, 'Please, God — please let me have this one thing. Can this be okay for me to have this one thing?' Even though I was wrestling with God, my relationship with Rachel was growing more serious. We contemplated her staying in the States on a more permanent basis and us getting an apartment together. We would go to gay bars just to have a place to be able to be affectionate with each other in public.

"We thought we had a good act going, disguising our relationship as just good, close friends, but my parents discerned differently. One day they sat her down and told her she had to leave. Needless to say, I was extremely sad after she left. Heartbroken.

"I am so thankful that my parents are Christians and could spiritually discern what was going on and took action. Rachel leaving the country was key. Again, the scales fell off my eyes and I then begged God, 'If I am single for the rest of my life and never have sex again, then fine, but please, please don't let me walk back into this again.'"

First Response

When a woman you have been meeting with, spending time with, or even began to disciple tells you she is struggling with lesbianism or same-sex attraction, immediately tell her you are proud of her for telling you and that you know how hard it was for her to bring this up. Reassure her that you're going to help her through this the best you can. She needs to know you are not going to abandon her or condemn her. You don't need to convince her that it is wrong. She knows that. She has either read it in the Bible, heard it from another Christian or even learned it in a sermon. She has most likely so shamed herself that it probably took all the guts she had to share it with you. So be quick to show compassion, love, and a sensitive heart.

In Over Your Head

At this point you may feel a bit in over your head. Your disciple has just shared a very deep and shameful piece of her life, and you may be the first person she has told. You are not going to be able to help her through this alone. She needs professional counsel. I would recommend you connecting her with a professional Christian counselor who is better equipped in this area. You can continue to walk beside her in this healing journey as a loving, caring friend. The rest of this chapter is extra information for your benefit but is not meant for making a diagnosis or to take the place of professional counseling.

Listen and Ask Questions

You want to listen to her journey and how she came to the point of confiding in you. So make up your mind to do a lot of listening and not a lot of talking (which is hard for me at times!). To help her get started, you could ask her questions such as "What made you decide to share this with me today?" or "How long have these thoughts been going on?" or "How do you feel about it?" or "Have you sought any other help?"

To find out what some of the root issues might be, you could ask about her family background, such as her relationship with her mother and her father. Many times the root issues can be traced back to one of these two relationships being severely troubled. Other root causes to lesbianism are childhood sexual abuse, physical or emotional trauma, skewed parental roles, and early exposure to pornography.

You can also ask her if there are other issues surrounding this one such as pornography (print and/or online), sexually explicit movies, etc. This will help you understand the depth of the struggle. The bottom line is to ask questions in a grace-filled way and listen with compassion. Again, reassure her you want to help the best you can.

Background Check

Much of the research I have done and many of the people I have interviewed or talked with about this chapter seemed to have in their background one of the issues listed below that made them more susceptible to temptations in this area. These factors are not exhaustive, and many times a unique combination of more than one is present:

* Not bonding properly to the same-sex parent

* Early exposure to pornography

* Sexual abuse

* Sexual experimentation

* Low or negative body image

* Overly identifying with the opposite-sex parent

* Media

According to Kermit Rainman in his article "An Overlooked Mission Field" in Focus on the Family Magazine, "Homosexuality is a relational problem driven by a deep need for love and affirmation from the same-sex gender. When the legitimate need for same-sex affirmation is not met during childhood development, the person may seek fulfillment in illegitimate ways — including homosexuality."

Change is Possible

Freedom from lesbianism, and same-sex attraction and fantasy, is increasingly experienced as women mature and deepen in their relationship with Jesus Christ. This transformation enables them to shed their old, sinful identity and in its place learn new ways of relating to themselves and others.

Change requires strong motivation, hard work, and perseverance. Hundreds of former lesbians have found a large degree of change — attaining abstinence from lesbian behaviors, lessening of lesbian temptations, strengthening their sense of feminine identity, and correcting distorted styles of relating with members of the same and opposite gender. Some former lesbians marry and some don't, but marriage is not the measuring stick; spiritual growth is.

How to Help

We cannot make anyone do something they don't want to do. Your disciple must be motivated herself to want to change. But you can play a very important part in assisting her in overcoming lesbianism.

If you are talking with a woman who wants to walk out of a lesbian lifestyle, and you discern she has never begun a personal relationship with Jesus, then start by sharing the gospel with her. Explain God's love for her, Christ's death on the cross, and that we are all sinners. Emphasize Christ's death on her behalf and the need for her to ask forgiveness of her sins and to trust Jesus to pay the penalty for those sins.

If you are helping a Christian struggling with this issue, you can pray that God will give her the courage and perseverance to achieve sexual abstinence. Sexual activity usually covers deep wounds. Once the activity stops, the "painkiller" of sex wears off and underlying emotional pain can surface. Be there to listen and support her in this process.

Pray that God will help her find biblical resolution to underlying issues that led to a lesbian orientation. Learn what you can about these problems, and find someone with expertise who can counsel your friend. Also pray that the Lord will help her reconnect with His original design and purpose for her as a woman. You can play a tremendous part in her healing just by being a role model of what a godly woman is like. That means being vulnerable about your weaknesses and seeking to grow in your relationship with Jesus Christ.

Don't discount your ability to help your disciple leave lesbianism and embrace all of God's plans for her life. Be a friend: encourage, confront, listen, and share. Go side by side with her through the challenging adventure ahead.

Information in these last two sections was largely gathered from www. exodus-international.org

Punishing Behaviors

"I'm a lesbian," Susan said, barely above a whisper.

She felt incredibly ashamed, I could see it in her face and my heart ached for her. I immediately told her I was proud of her and was glad she had told me. We talked at length that afternoon about her journey, how she had been in a relationship with a woman for years and how it had recently ended. Susan had put her faith in Christ earlier that year and desired to walk with God and give Him every area of her life.

Sadly, when she was young, she stumbled upon her dad's huge stash of Playboy magazines. As she viewed the materials, she internalized the fact that if this was what her father desired, she would desire it as well. Fantasizing about the naked women she saw in the magazines, she grew up having a sexual attraction to women, which later resulted in a full-scale lesbian lifestyle.

I listed to Susan's story with compassion. She cried a few times as she talked. I realized that the help she was going to need was way out of my league when she began to explain how she punished herself. "I hate myself for thinking this way and for being a lesbian. I punish myself for it in hopes I will not give into the temptations anymore," Susan said.

She went on to tell me how she regularly put small pieces of broken glass in her shoes, near her small toes, and walked around with the glass cutting into her feet all day to punish herself for her actions.

Praying for, guiding and encouraging a person struggling to be free of lesbianism was going to be challenging enough. Add on self-mutilation, and I knew I was not equipped to give her the help she needed.

"Susan, I cannot believe the pain and turmoil you have carried for so long," I said. "You have taken a courageous step today by sharing with me your inner battle. I would like for you to consider getting professional help in this area. I want to continue to meet with you regularly, to talk and pray, but I am confident that I don't have all the necessary skills to help you see true freedom in this area of your life."

I later went to the Christian bookstore in my area and bought her the book Coming Out of Homosexuality, by Bob Davies and Lori Rentzel, and gave it to her the next time we got together. She began to do some research on her own, and soon began to see a Christian counselor who had helped many men and women come out of this lifestyle.

So if you at any point feel over your head in a particular situation, don't feel like you have to help the person alone. You can continue to be a source of encouragement, prayer, and a sounding board while they are getting professional help.

From Jamie's Perspective

As I talked more with Jamie, whom I introduced you to at the beginning of this chapter, about her journey in her struggle with lesbianism, I asked her what, in her opinion, were the important steps to remember when a person wants to change. Below are the main ideas she presented:

Got to Want It

The person in the lesbian life style needs to want to get out of it. The woman has most likely shared her struggle with you because she does want to be free of it. But even after she shares it with you, she has to, at a heart level, want to be free. "The longer a person is in it, the harder it is to get out," Jamie said, "because the whole life becomes immersed in it (politically, relationally, etc.), and the longer you are in that lifestyle, the more and more your mind becomes warped and darkened."

Immediately Break Off the Relationship

If the woman you are talking with is in a lesbian relationship, she needs to immediately break off all ties with the other woman, even if the other woman is a Christian. Do not talk, email or phone for at least six months. There will still be chemistry and feelings, so the need for total separation is the only way to gain perspective. If the other woman wants to keep the relationship, then change your phone number and email to give yourself time to heal and think. "In a lesbian relationship," Jamie said, "the conscience becomes seared, and it takes time to begin to heal the conscience."

No Going Back

There is really no going back. If the woman you are discipling/meeting with, or the other woman in the relationship, wants to be friends again, your disciple needs to consider the motives behind that desire. Going back to a friendship only opens the door for temptation in the future. This is not what is needed for a woman trying to walk out of these patterns.

Replace the Habit

The discipler needs to encourage the woman to get involved in other things such as Bible study, new activities, and new friends. The discipler can't take on the time replacement that the disciple will feel when her lesbian relationship is over, so she needs to connect her with others to fill that time gap and emptiness she will most likely feel.

Professional Christian Counseling

In counseling, the woman can better work towards understanding the root issue behind her lesbian lifestyle or tendencies. Many people think they are lesbian when in reality they are masking a deeper problem of pain in their life. "Lesbianism is reactionary," Jamie said, "meaning that something else has happened, whether it be sexual abuse, or maternal or paternal neglect." Working through underlying relational and abuse problems is a significant component in this process. Making use of individual and pastoral counseling, support groups, personal Bible study, and same-sex discipleship groups are also beneficial.

Be Sensitive to Her Broken Heart

Don't dismiss the fact that a significant relationship in her life has ended and that she is most likely devastated over it. She has a broken heart, and you as the discipler need to be sensitive to that. Ask her questions, talk with her, and be compassionate.

Accountability

The woman may still feel chemistry at times, even after a long season of abstaining from lesbian relationships. "I still feel chemistry sometimes," Jamie said. "I pray immediately to God to please help me with that and to help me not do that again. I have told my friends about these struggles, and they pray for me and hold me accountable. I have even told them what it would look like if I began to lie to them and what are the warning signs that I am slipping, so they can help me when I am weak."

Additional Resources

Here are some books anyone struggling with lesbianism or same-sex attractions would find helpful:

Restoring Sexual Identity: Hope for Women Who Struggle With Same-Sex Attraction, Anne Paulk

Re-Igniting The Hope For Homosexuals, John and Anne Paulk

Out of Egypt; One Woman's Journey Out of Lesbianism, Jeanette Howard

Coming out of Homosexuality, Bob Davies and Lori Rentzel

The Heart of the Matter: Roots and Causes of Female Homosexuality, Dr. Joseph Nicolosi

Helping People Step Out of Homosexuality, Frank Worthen

Some websites I've found very beneficial when helping people through this issue are:

www.exodusinternational.org

www.lovewonout.com

www.focusonthefamily.org

In Summary

Sexual abuse, maternal or paternal neglect, early exposure to pornography, and distorted sexual temptations can lead women to experiment, engage in, and adopt lesbianism as a lifestyle. Unfortunately, the longer a woman is engaged in this lifestyle, the harder it is to leave it, as her entire life is immersed in the homosexual culture and distorted ways of thinking. A Christian woman struggling with lesbianism often feels a tremendous amount of shame and guilt, and at times hopelessness. We as disciplers can be a tremendous source of hope and caring as we point our disciples to the resources they need to find real help in this area.

Sexual Abuse: "I'll never tell…"

"My first abuser was my babysitter's husband," Carla said. "He began sexually abusing me when I was 3, and it continued until I was 5. He started by touching me and fondling me. It grew to him making me fondle him and oral sex (him to me). No penetration ever took place — just the touching, fondling, and oral sex. It was expected. I had no choice in the matter, it was something he made me do, it was quick, and when it was over, he acted as if nothing ever happened. And I felt so ashamed; I swore to myself, I'll never tell…

"My innocence was stolen, and it was as if men knew it and took advantage of me when I was by myself. I remember one day I went with my dad to get a haircut. I asked him if I could go buy some candy next door and he said yes. As I went to the checkout counter with my licorice the old man behind the counter came around to me and put his hand on my bottom. I ran as fast as I could out of that store, back to my dad, and never told a soul. The next abuser was a neighbor, and then when I was in high school I was date-raped."

Sexual abuse has injured countless women's lives. If you disciple a woman who has been through any form of sexual abuse, at some point she will need to begin the painful process of working through what has happened. As disciplers, we can be agents of love and listening, while speaking the truth about God and her true biblical identity as she goes though the healing process.

First Response

When a woman you have been discipling shares with you that she has been sexually abused, immediately tell her you are proud of her for telling you and that you know how hard it was for her to bring this up. Reassure her that you're going to help her through this the best you can. Because of the overwhelming guilt she feels, which will be discussed later in the chapter, your first words need to be, "I am so sorry that happened to you. That was not your fault; you were the victim."

In Over Your Head

At this point you may feel a bit in over your head. Your disciple has just shared a very traumatic event in her life, and you may be the first person she has told since the event took place. You are not going to be able to help her through this alone. She needs professional counsel. I would recommend you connect her with a Christian counselor who is better equipped in this area. You can continue to walk beside her in this healing journey as a loving, caring friend, but if you try to be the one and only person in her life to help her through this, you may end up harming the healing process, as you most likely don't have the experience or education necessary to really help. I don't either! The rest of this chapter is extra information for your benefit but is not meant for making a diagnosis or for taking the place of professional counseling.

Facts About Sexual Abuse

Repeated Abuse (Victimization) — More often than not, women who have been abused will be abused again. Whether it is repeated sexual abuse by different people, date rape, etc., sexual abuse usually is not a one-time event.

Shame and Guilt — Tragically, no matter how young the woman was when she was sexually abused, she feels as if she could have stopped it. Even if she was extremely young and there was no possible way she could have stopped the abuse, she still feels as if she should have or could have. She berates herself that she didn't say no, that she didn't run and didn't go tell someone. She blames herself for the abuse, and this heaps shame and guilt on the hurt and pain already present. This is the bottom-line reason why women do not share their abuse — they think they could have stopped it, and therefore feel extreme guilt and shame.

Red Flags

Here are some of the more common red flags that can indicate a woman might have been sexually abused at some point in her life. Not all of these will be present, and this list is not exhaustive.

Fear of Intimacy — The woman fears that if she lets someone too close, he or she will find out the secret of the abuse she has tried their entire life to keep hidden.

Inability to Trust — The woman was not able to trust the person who did this to her, so it is difficult for her to trust anybody, as she feels her trust may be taken advantage of.

Control Issues — The woman feels like she must be in control of every area because she was not in control in her abusive situation.

Weight and Eating Issues — A woman with abuse in her past will either desire to be overweight so as to look bad and possibly keep abuse from reoccurring, or might be incredibly thin or have a very tight control over what she eats, as she was not in control while being abused.

Incredible Insecurity — She might even stay in a bad, abusive relationship just to feel secure.

Deflects Conversation Away from Herself — to keep the big secret hidden.

Displaced Anger — Deep down she is very angry and bitter at the abuse and abuser, and possibly herself. She has so deeply stuffed the abuse and kept it hidden that the anger will show itself in other ways.

Overly Flirts with Men — Because of her abuse, this distortion was burned into her heart and mind at a young age.

Incredibly Sexual — Many women who have been abused have reacted sexually to the point of bisexual encounters and lesbianism. When a woman's sexuality has been distorted, it's hard to find pleasure.

Talking About It Further

Only if you feel comfortable and if she wants to talk more about it with you, ask her if she would like to further share the sexual abuse in her history. She will most likely begin to weep, and nod her head yes, and again, you need to reiterate that you are so sorry this happened to her. Remind her again that she was a victim, she is precious, she did not bring it on, and she did not deserve it.

Explain to your disciple that as painful as it may be, God wants her to be free, and one of the ways we find freedom is by speaking out loud, bringing into the light, hidden and hurtful things. Gently let her tell you what happened. Remember, because of victimization, it is likely the abuse happened more than once.

If your disciple desires to share more, here are a few questions you can ask to help her draw her out:

* How often did the abuse happen?

* How many people have abused you throughout the years?

* Is the abuse still going on?

* How are your relationships with men? Women?

* Are you ready to give this to the Lord?

* Are you ready for God to come in and heal?

* Are you ready to open dark areas and reveal things that are hidden?

If your disciple is not willing to talk about her abuse, you don't want to force her. You could ask her if she would feel more comfortable talking to a professional counselor and that you will help make that connection happen if she would like. Whatever the case may be, she will eventually need to talk about it to begin her healing. You can reassure her that when she is ready to share, you will be there to listen. Assure her of your prayers for her.

"Why, God?"

Many women might wonder why God let this happen to them. Let them vent; let them share; let them weep. If she is really looking to you to give her an answer, you can respond with, "I don't know why this happened to you, but I do know that God wants you to be free, and He will deal with that person." You can also add, "God did not want this to happen, and He loves you and will help you through this."

Our Role

Again, your disciple needs professional counsel. As you walk through the process with her, pray for her, affirm her, and let her know that no matter what happens, you will be there to listen and to unconditionally love her. There is a part of her that expects to be rejected, and you need to be a constant friend and voice of truth in her life. She needs a gentle, constant reminder of God's good will for her, His love for her, and that He sees her as precious and beloved. You can brainstorm together encouraging Scriptures about healing, her identity in Christ, and God's love for her.

Steps for Healing

Carla went through the difficult work it took to begin the process of healing in this area. She is now a thriving woman of God and uses the things that happened to her to help other women. I asked her to outline for me the steps that helped her as she walked out of this wounded place in her life. Here are many of the things she shared:

"Healing begins when we bring things that are hidden in our lives and speak them into the light. Dark things need to be brought into the light to be exposed. We need to purge things in our lives that are making us sick. We need to speak out everything in our lives so that there are no dark places anymore. Healing comes from the inside out; we have got to give it to God. Complete honesty with God and others is paramount for healing. Shame keeps things hidden and unhealed. Satan has no power when we bring things into the light."

Relationship with the Lord

A relationship with the Lord is the first step. If you are not sure that the woman who has revealed her past to you is a Christian, begin by sharing with her the gospel of Jesus Christ. "My relationship with God was key to my healing," Carla said. "I knew God was there and that He was sorry. He knew about it and He was going to handle it."

Prayer

As disciplers, we need to pray for the women in our lives we suspect have been sexually abused — that they would come to the place where they are willing to talk about what happened, bring it into the light, give it to God, and begin the painful process of healing. We can pray for them as they open up to us that the Lord would remind them of things they have stuffed away, so they can share those memories and not stuff them anymore.

Admit It Happened

At some point, the woman you are helping needs to admit (out loud) that the abuse actually happened. She's got to speak it, own it, and embrace that it happened. She has to come to the place where she is not hiding it anymore. She has to say, "Yes, this happened to me."

Admit Someone Was Wrong

Making excuses for someone, or blaming yourself, hinders the healing process. The woman who has been sexually abused needs to admit that what was done to her was wrong and that the person who took advantage of her was wrong.

Embrace the Truth

A woman who has been sexually abused needs to embrace the truth about who she is in Christ — that she is worthy, lovely, and a new creation in Christ. She can have a fresh start. One step in embracing truth about her true identity is to read the Bible and highlight every verse that talks about our blessings and position as adopted children of God. I would recommend she commit her favorites to memory.

Reject Lies

Women who have been abused may think they will always be victims and will never be free, so they think, "Why try to change?" Satan has sown a pack of lies to these women to the tune that they think they are worthless, used up, and that God is not watching out for them. We can help our disciples counter these lies by rejecting these thoughts and replacing them with Scripture.

Additional Help

This chapter just begins to uncover some of the many issues involved when a woman has been sexually abused. I hope it has given you a place to begin walking with your disciple toward complete healing in this area of her life. If you need additional help, please utilize some of the resources below:

Rape, Abuse & Incense National Network: www.rainn.org (lists different types of sexual abuse, getting help and an online hotline)

After Silence: www.aftersilence.org (a non profit organization, message board and chat room for sexual abuse survivors and victims)

Way2Hope: www.way2hope.org/sexabuse.htm (learn about, prevent and recover from the various forms of sexual abuse)

The Wounded Heart: Hope for Adult Victims of Childhood Abuse, Dr. Dan B. Allender

Overcoming Sexual Abuse: Practical Help for Adult Survivors, Bob Davies and Lori Rentzel

Healing Victims of Sexual Abuse, Paula Sandford

Learning to Trust Again: A Young Woman's Journey of Healing from Sexual Abuse, Christa Sands

Changes that Heal, Dr. Henry Cloud

Who I Am in Christ, Neil Anderson

In Summary

When a woman is abused sexually, her identity becomes distorted, and she often instinctively hides what has happened. Tragically, even if a woman was extremely young, she feels like she could have stopped it, which just adds to the guilt and shame. As disciplers, we can be agents of love and listening while speaking the truth about God and her true biblical identity as she goes through the healing process. Understanding common red flags of a woman who might have been abused in her past, referring her to professional counsel, and being patient as she begins to reveal the hurt, guilt and shame, can greatly aid her in overcoming the abuse and even in helping other women in the future.

 **ISSUE #6**

Comparison: "I wish I looked like her..."

Many women struggle with comparison in some form or another. As disciplers, we need to help the women in our lives reject the whispers of comparison and embrace the destiny they have been created for.

Comparing Weaknesses to Strengths

Each of us has strengths and weaknesses. For example, I cannot sing. I can't. I know this; it's just true. I mean I do sing in church, in my car, etc., but trust me — I know I could never make a living singing. I do enjoy theater and acting, and was involved in the theater arts department throughout junior high and high school. I went to college on a theater scholarship. But when it came to auditioning for musicals, I never even tried for the lead part. The reason I even explain all this is because one thing I have learned over the years is to not compare my weakness (in this case singing) to another person's strength.

Oftentimes you may hear your disciple compare a weakness of hers to another's strength. She may say, "I wish I could dance like her," when she is an incredible piano player, or "I wish I was as smart as she is," when she is an incredible athlete. When you hear your disciple make comments about another woman in any area, remind her that she has strengths as well (be specific — list what they are), and encourage her not to compare her weaknesses with another person's strengths, because if she does, she will always be disappointed.

Common Areas of Comparison

Looks — wanting another person's face, nose, body, height, hair, etc. I always wanted long, thick hair so I could pull it up in a messy bun. There was even one year I had three spiral perms to try and achieve this look. All it did was absolutely fry my hair, and I had to cut it off (very short!).

Career — wanting another woman's career. Many women have been able to advance to top-level positions in their career and get much respect and can yield a great deal of authority in their spheres of influence.

Family — desiring another woman's family life. We compare our family, kids, and our marriage to other women's families and seem to come up with the short stick. The problem with this, of course, is that we usually don't know what is really going on in another woman's life at all.

Singleness/Marriage — Some women with difficult marriages and overwhelming child responsibilities can look at a single woman's life with envy. Oh, to be able to do whatever you want, to take naps whenever you want, to not have to think about every decision and how it will affect your spouse... Then, of course, the single woman may look to the married woman's life and wish for a spouse, someone to live life with, and a busy home.

Spiritual Life — desiring the walk with God that another woman has. We long to have learned all the lessons, have the prayer life, the witnessing abilities, the ministry of another woman, an so on. Oftentimes another woman's spiritual life was gained by enduing trials that made her stronger and seemingly closer to God.

Social Status — Whether it's the neighborhood a friend lives in, the title she has, who her parents are, or who she knows, many women desire a different social status.

Intelligence — desiring to be as smart as the next person. I remember in college having to study weeks before an exam, while other friends of mine barely did any of the reading and could ace a test.

Financial Security — desiring to have the financial resources of another woman. I remember talking with one of the women I discipled a few years ago. I walked into her room and she was flipping through a car catalogue.

"What's up, Kelly?" I said.

"Oh, nothing, I am just deciding what car I want. My parents said I could have any car I wanted up to $40,000 when I graduate at the end of this semester."

My jaw dropped open. I said, "What are you going to do with the SUV you already have?"

"Oh, I don't know — probably keep it and use it as my second car…"

God's Word

The Bible speaks to this comparison throughout the Bible. We are not to covet what others have, instead having hearts that are thankful and joyful in what we have been given. In this familiar passage we see Peter, one of Jesus' disciples, comparing himself to John, another disciple:

> "Peter turned and saw that the disciple whom Jesus loved was following them. (This was the one who had leaned back against Jesus at the supper and had said, "Lord, who is going to betray you?") When Peter saw him, he asked, "Lord, what about him?" Jesus answered, "If I want him to remain alive until I return, what is that to you? You must follow me" (John 21:20-22, NIV).

Peter needed to follow Christ and keep his eyes on Him and not be distracted in his mission by comparing his life with anyone else's. What a good word for us and our disciples. The moment we begin to look at someone else — in any way — and compare our lives, we have taken our eyes off Jesus and His purpose and mission for our own lives.

Hardships Make Us Stronger

Some things in our lives have made us stronger. There are countless things in our lives that we would have changed if we could have. Among the many things I would have changed, if given the chance, would have been the money situation growing up — the fact that we never had any. At age 13 I began to work in my parents' restaurant as a dishwasher. Ever since that day, I have always had at least one job. I worked not just to have extra spending money, but also to buy things I needed, such as lunch at school each day, school clothes, etc. Yes, I would have changed having to be a dishwasher at 13. But looking back now, I can see how working helped make me stronger as a person and develop a good work ethic. I appreciated things growing up and took meticulous care of games, clothes, etc., because in many cases I had paid for them myself.

If your disciple seems to complain often about hardship in her life, ask her what she thinks going though that hardship will produce in her life that will be helpful one day. You could also share how something you have had to go though has helped make you stronger.

The Blessing of Brown Eyes

A Chance to Die, the biography of Amy Carmichael written by Elizabeth Elliot, includes an incredible story of comparison. Amy was born with brown eyes and hated them, and as a young girl, she always wanted to have blue eyes. She would constantly pray to God, asking Him to change her brown eyes to blue.

When Amy was older, she became a missionary in India, rescuing hundreds of young girls from temple prostitution. She rescued these young girls by disguising herself, covering her body and hair like the other women in India with only her eyes showing. Her brown eyes made her look like other Indian women entering the temple, and so she was let in without hassle. She would then help the girls escape, bringing them to a safe place away from the temple.

She then began to understand that if God would have answered her prayers to have blue eyes, she would have been found out as a foreigner and not been able to fulfill the destiny for which God had fashioned her.

Embracing Your Own Destiny

My body, my personality, my laugh, my quirks, my family are all a part of my destiny and the unique purpose for which God has called me. God has a plan for me, and the way I look, and the talents and gifts I have been given by Him all help me fulfill that unique calling:

> "For I know the plans I have for you, declares the Lord. Plans to prosper you and not to harm you, plans to give you hope and a future. Then you will call upon me and come and pray to me, and I will listen to you. You will seek me and find me when you seek me with all of your heart" (Jeremiah 29:11-13, NIV).

> "All the days ordained for me were written in your book before one of them came to be" (Psalm 139:16, NIV).

Now let's just say that I was younger and looked different. Instead of 5'2", let's say I was 5'6". Let's say I had breast augmentation and had tons of money to buy beautiful gowns, get plastic surgery and travel all over the country competing in different beauty pageants. I could maybe, possibly, with all the best coaches, have (long shot) become Miss America. And that would be great, and I could have shared Christ with the women I met in that arena. But then who would live out the destiny that Lori Joiner was supposed to live out? Who would have led Sara, Gina, and Kathie to Christ? Who would have established the Faith House? Who would have written this book about discipleship? I was meant to live out this life I have had, to fulfill this destiny — not another one.

So if your disciple constantly compares herself to others and wishes for something different than what she has, reassure her that God has a unique calling for her and that who she is (what she looks like, etc.) is part of that calling. He has a purpose for which he has created you and her. So together take inventory of each of your strengths and weaknesses, and thank God for them. Thank Him for making you exactly the way you are and for the unique calling He has for you to live out.

Additional Resources

The Search for Significance, Robert McGee

Personality Plus, Florence Littauer

In Summary

Whether your disciple is comparing her looks, her spiritual life, or her stage of life, issues of comparison need to be identified and covered by God's Word. The root of comparison is insecurity about who we are and who God has made us. The result is that we might not take hold of the purpose God has for us, always seeing the grass greener on the other side. When we fully embrace that we have been created for a purpose and a destiny, and that our looks, personality, gifts and life experiences all play into God's plan for us, we will stop trying to live out someone else's destiny and move forward in our own.

 **ISSUE #7**

Imagination: "A woman's thoughts can be her ally or enemy…"

"I just don't know if I am really a Christian," Lisa said as we sat outside a McDonald's in the Middle East. We were both on a mission trip together, and as we took a break from our ministry to get a caramel ice cream, she confided this to me.

"Why don't you think you are a Christian?" I replied.

"Well, I am just not sure I really meant it when I prayed."

"Have you trusted him to pay for your sins? Have you asked him to be your Lord and Savior?" I inquired.

"Yes, Lisa replied, "I have done that a hundred times, but I am just not sure. I do good for a while, then these doubts start creeping back in my mind and I begin to wonder if I really meant it the last time I did it, so I do it again. And it is hard for me to tell others about Jesus when I always doubt if I am really a Christian."

Countless women have destructive thought patterns that are truly holding them back in life. Lisa's story above was just that. She was a Christian. She wanted Jesus to forgive her, and had trusted in Him and His saving work on the cross on her behalf. She wanted Him to be her Savior and Lord and meant it with all her heart. The problem was that at some point she began to doubt herself, she embraced this doubt, she thought about the doubt, she pondered the doubt, and the more she entertained the doubt, the more she hung onto the doubt and the more she believed it. She hated the doubting feelings. But it was a habit for her to think on them. Like chain smoking, once a thought entered her mind, it was like a temptation she could not say no to. She would think on the thoughts so long and deeply that she would eventually conclude that she was indeed not a Christian and then be in fear that if she did not put her faith in Christ again, she would go to hell.

A woman's thoughts can be her ally as well as her enemy. Many times we develop habits of destructive thought patterns that can hinder our walk with God. Identifying these patterns in your disciple's life and helping her develop more healthy thought patterns will be instrumental in her relationship with God and her relationships with others.

Thought patterns such as sexual fantasies, worries, fears, degradation toward self, doubts, jealousy, and unforgiveness are just a few. One woman's father had left her mother for another woman, and it understandably devastated her. For years she held onto unforgiveness toward her father, and sadly, that pain was doing her much damage as the bitterness grew in her heart. While the act was very sad (the father leaving the family for someone else), she was stuck and not moving forward in her Christian growth. She would constantly think through a cycle of thoughts: 1) he left my mom, 2) he left me, 3) how could he leave me and our family for someone else? 4) he must not have loved me, 5) he said he loved me, 6) He must have been lying, 7) I will never forgive him for the hurt he caused, 8) I hate him for the pain he caused us...

Some days she would be so busy in life that she would not walk through this cycle of thoughts. Other days, though, she was completely overwhelmed and controlled by the thoughts and the accompanying pain they brought.

The answer is not to stop thinking altogether, obviously. God has given us incredible minds and imaginations to use for His glory. Many of the wonderful programs, missions, and inventions we have are because we have amazing, God-given imaginations to think and create. The answer is to cultivate a mind that thinks upon delightful topics such as hopes, plans, future goals and Scripture. We need to develop in ourselves and the women we disciple incredible imaginations that might just hold the next great ideas for our generation — ideas to help the extreme poor, end world hunger, help orphans, etc. We need to recognize destructive thought patterns and steer our disciples' imaginations (and ours) Godward!

Crush Cycle

One area of my own life that continuously occupied my thoughts were crushes on guys. Crushes are imaginations running wild with thoughts about a certain guy. After many years of crushes, most of them well documented in my many journals, I thought about the anatomy of a crush and wrote down (in a circle) each stage of a crush. I remember very well sitting in a meeting and writing this down on a note pad. I then began to try to stop myself from future crushes by recognizing where I was in the crush cycle and stopping it there. I have since shared the drawing and stages of a crush with countless women in an effort to educate (even humorously) about the stages of a crush so as to keep our hearts from getting crushed over and over.

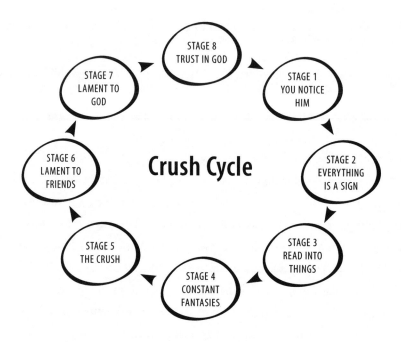

Stage One: You Notice Him

He has the looks you desire, the personality you have wished for, the status you admire. You decide he is the one for you, and all you have to do now is get him to notice you.

Stage Two: Everything Is a Sign

He has the same Bible as you, he has a little sister as do you, he likes coffee ice cream (wow, so do you!). He is strong where you are weak and vice versa. And you both end up in the same Sunday school class (or on the same mission trip, etc.). It just couldn't be more God's plan, you think, as you interpret each of the above items as a sign from God that he is the one.

Stage Three: Read into Things

When he opens the door for you, says hello, or offers a ride, you take each of these polite gestures as a sign that he likes you and will soon be asking you out on a date.

Stage Four: Constant Fantasies

You keep yourself up at night wondering, How will I respond when he asks me out on our date, what should I wear, how should I accept the invite? Should I say, "Oh, yes, that sounds great," or "Yes, I would love to"? Is a December wedding pushing it, or should I wait for spring? White dress or ivory, strapless or off the shoulder? I wonder what my wedding night would be like with him — Victoria's Secret or Fredrick's of Hollywood?" Is anyone relating to me yet?

Stage Five: The Crush

For whatever reason, the crush happens. Maybe the mission trip is over and he never asked you out. Maybe the project at work is finished and he never indicated his feelings to you. Perhaps one of you moves. Or, in one of my crush stories, he asks out your friend instead of you!

Stage Six: Lament to Friends

I remember one year on the Fourth of July weeping my heart out about some guy I had a huge crush on. He had asked out my friend on a date after I had decided that he was clearly God's choice for me. My friends consoled me, patted me on the back, and told me God had someone else for me. I sought out any friend I could to console me, have pity on my broken heart, and listen to me tell the stories of this one-sided relationship over and over.

Stage Seven: Lament to God

After I had exhausted my friends with my weeping and self-pity, I then turned to the Holy Spirit. I wish I could say I went to God before going to my friends, but that was not the case. As I grow in my relationship with Him, this does happen more often. The good thing is that God never tires of my broken heart, even when I do it to myself. He cares about me and is close to the brokenhearted.

Stage Eight: Trust in God

Vow to trust God and not run ahead in your imagination about a certain guy. Decide to remain friends with men in your heart and mind until they communicate a desire for more. Vow not to go through the crush cycle over and over and over. At this final stage I re-ask the Holy Spirit to take the driver's seat in my life. I ask the Holy Spirit to fill me up to overflowing, to give me the mind of Christ and the heart of Christ, and to help me stay focused on the tasks He has for me at that point instead of wasting a lot of emotional energy on something that may never happen.

Replace

I have found it helpful in my life to replace negative thought patterns with new, healthy ones. For example, I used to worry about money. When I was in college I constantly thought of how I was going to pay for that next semester of college, or how would I pay for books, or what I would do if my car broke down or if I got sick and could not work my college job, or if I had to quit school to work — and on it went. While none of these things ever happened, I constantly worried about them. Whether walking to class, lying in my bed at night, or trying to study, this thought pattern of the fear of not having enough money was never far from my mind. I would be having a great day, and then the thoughts would start, and a downward spiral would take place in my heart and mind. The fear at times seemed overwhelming.

To replace this fear-of-money cycle I felt trapped in, I began to read Scripture and memorize verses that explained how God is my provider and how He loves me and knows what I need before I even ask Him. I began to memorize verses about faith and having faith in God and not dwelling on fear. So each time I would begin to think of the fears of not enough money, I would start saying Scriptures to myself, and I would pray and give God my worries. Slowly I was able to replace a negative, fearful thought pattern with one about God's faithfulness to provide for me. I would much rather think on God and His love for me than fear having no money to pay my bills.

Here are a few steps that will help identify and replace negative thought patterns:

If each time you are with your disciple, she is bringing up the same worry, ask her more about it. Ask her to explain what she is thinking. Ask how often she thinks about this and how it affects her mood or view of God. It might be a well-established thought pattern, and she may be unaware of its effects on her, her relationship with God, and with others.

Ask if she would like for you to help her brainstorm other things to think on, particularly Bible verses that reveal truth about that situation for her to think upon when she is tempted to dwell on the other.

You could brainstorm together and pray together. You could even share a thought pattern you would like to replace, and she could help you brainstorm verses.

The next time you get together or see each other, ask how it is going — how you both are doing at saying no to the old negative thoughts and embracing new things to think on that honor God and speak scriptural truth to the situation.

We Are Not Alone

God has given us much to help us in the pursuit of a healthy imagination. Whether your disciple is battling self-degrading thought patterns, jealous thoughts, bitter thoughts, or sexual thoughts, we can take heart that we are not alone in this battle for our imaginations. First of all, we have the Holy Spirit Himself living inside of us. He is our teacher and counselor and will help us from the inside out. When we are tempted to think whatever thought we are trying to battle, He will give us another option, helping us escape and think on other things. We also have the Word of God. Scripture is full of verses that help us in this area. God Himself shows us things we ought to think upon.

Consider these verses and perhaps commit a few to memory:

"Those who live according to the sinful nature have their minds set on what that nature desires; but those who live in accordance with the Spirit have their minds set on what the Spirit desires" (Romans 8:5, NIV).

"Since, then, you have been raised with Christ, set your hearts on things above, where Christ is seated at the right hand of God. Set your minds on things above, not on earthly things" (Colossians 3:1,2, NIV).

"Therefore, holy brothers, who share in the heavenly calling, fix your thoughts on Jesus, the apostle and high priest whom we confess" (Hebrews 3:1, NIV).

"So we fix our eyes not on what is seen, but on what is unseen. For what is seen is temporary, but what is unseen is eternal" (2 Corinthians 4:18, NIV).

"Finally, brothers, whatever is true, whatever is noble, whatever is right, whatever is pure, whatever is lovely, whatever is admirable — if anything is excellent or praiseworthy — think about such things" (Philippians 4:8, NIV).

Another great help is our relationship with our disciples and other Christian women. If we let our struggles be known, if we tell someone that this is an area of weakness for us, then others know how to pray and encourage us. They will know where we are weak and can help us during those times we are especially tempted to put ourselves through a "crush cycle" or "doubt cycle" or "unforgiveness cycle."

Take Inventory

There are many things that can hinder a healthy thought life and make it even harder not to let our mind run rampant with fantasies of all types. In my own life I have found it helpful to monitor what I let into my mind and heart through various forms of entertainment such as certain types of TV shows, music, movies, and books. I am not saying that all of these media forms are bad; I am suggesting that oftentimes they can have an effect on what we think about later.

If you or your disciple is struggling with sexual thoughts, for example, perhaps you need to take inventory of the programming and movies being watched, books and magazines being read, or websites being visited. Are they chock-full of sex scenes and lustful situations? Perhaps you both may be hindering your desire for purity in this area by what you are letting into your minds.

Think on These Things

Consider good things to think upon. Again, it is not bad to dream, imagine, etc., as long as the things we are dreaming about are good, lovely, and praiseworthy. As I stated earlier, God has given us incredible imaginations to use for His kingdom. Ask him to help give you thoughts that are from above, or to dream a dream through you — perhaps you will imagine a new way to help people, feed children, or reduce poverty. You may have a special idea about something that God wants to do through you. On that, my sister, fantasize away!

Here are a few questions you and your disciple could cover together as you talk deeper about this area of your lives:

* ❖ What are you tending to focus on lately?

* ❖ Are you struggling with any fantasies (sexual, hateful, etc.) that could be hindering your growing relationship with God?

* ❖ What do the verses (listed earlier) say we are to focus on?

* ❖ What is the common theme in all those verses?

* ❖ How can you shift your focus to the things mentioned in those verses?

Additional Resources

Power Thoughts: 12 Strategies to Win the Battle of the Mind, Joyce Meyer

Battle Field of the Mind, Joyce Meyer

Every Thought Captive: Battling the Toxic Beliefs that Separate Us from the Life We Crave, Jerusha Clark

In Summary

You and the women you disciple can be free from thought patterns and destructive thought cycles that may be hindering you from living for God and keeping your thoughts focused on him. God has given you His Holy Spirit, His Word, and Christian believers to help you let go of negative, harmful thoughts and free you and your disciple to live and walk closely with Him. Furthermore, God wants to use our imaginations to dream new dreams through us to further His kingdom in our lifetimes!

 **ISSUE #8**

Depression: "I'm not valuable to anyone…"

"God, take me to heaven if this is all there is," Tracy whispered to God at a particularly low time in her struggle with depression. "I did not want to take my own life," she told me. "I just didn't feel like living anymore if this pain was all there was going to be in my life.

"Looking back, I went through periods of depression but did not know it at the time. I remember not being able to get out of bed; I would try to distract myself from the overwhelming sense of dread in my life by watching movies, but even those did not help after a while. I would surf the internet for hours and watch movie trailers — anything to bring me joy or pleasure, but nothing worked, and the continual sense of dread would not go away."

Tracy and I were sitting in a restaurant talking, each with a cup of coffee in our hands. I asked to talk with her about her journey with depression that I had witnessed firsthand over the previous couple of years. I wanted, though, to talk about it deeper, so I could truly understand her and what had gone on in her mind, heart, and body through that dark season.

"I felt like a cloud followed me around," Tracy said. "I had a lack of motivation to do anything and there was no joy in life. I felt really alone, no one really understood how incredibly low I felt, and even if they could understand, I reasoned, how could they help?

"Being a Christian put a different spin on depression for me. It brought about a level of shame and guilt that was hard to deal with. I felt like a hypocrite. I would tell others the truth of God's Word but not really believe it for myself. The Bible felt hollow, and I had a hard time believing that what I read in the Bible was truly meant for me. I felt like the Lord was distant and I felt utterly hopeless. My best friend from college and I talked about things often, and at one point she said, 'Tracy, this isn't just a bad mood you are going to snap out of. You aren't snapping out of it. This is deeper, more of a pattern. I think you should talk to someone.'"

In Over Your Head

Depression is painful. It is a gradual process of shutting down inwardly and isolating one's self from people and the normal routines of life, which may lead to a desire to end life altogether. Depression can be caused by a chemical imbalance, a reaction to difficult and overwhelming life circumstances, or a mix of both. This chapter deals with such issues as helping your disciple realize that she is valuable and that God has a purpose for her life, steering her toward the medication or professional help she may need, and helping her regain joy and hope for the future. I have also included information about depression for your own understanding as the discipler, because unless you have gone through this yourself or have known a loved one going through this, you can run the risk of dismissing depression as just a sad mood that the woman needs to snap out of. This information is for your benefit and for you to gain understanding and insight. Don't feel the need to diagnose or treat your disciple. Walk through this season with her and point her to the professional help she needs.

Understanding Depression and Depressive Disorders

According to the National Institute of Mental Health (NIMH), a depressive disorder is an illness that involves the body, mood, and thoughts. It affects the way a woman eats and sleeps, the way she feels about herself, and the way she thinks. A depressive disorder is not the same as a passing blue mood. It is not a sign of personal weakness or a condition that can be willed or wished away. Women with a depressive illness cannot merely "pull themselves together" and get better. Without treatment, symptoms can last for weeks, months, or years. Appropriate treatment, however, can help most women who suffer from depression.

Causes of Depression

How does this happen? What can be done to stop it? If you have ever dealt with depression, you only wish you could have clear-cut answers to those questions. Because if you knew how it happened, perhaps you could then make it stop-for you or for someone you care about. Unfortunately, the causes of depression are deep and can be a combination of several different things. Some of the leading causes of depression are a family history of depression; being prone to low self-esteem; a pessimistic view of life and self, physical changes and illnesses such as stroke, heart attack and cancer; serious losses such as of a loved one; financial problems; and relational issues. There are no easy answers and no quick fixes.

In the book *Happiness is a Choice*, Frank Minrith and Paul Meier add a few more causes to this list such as attacks of Satan, working in our self-effort instead of relying on God, having wrong priorities, and repressed anger.

Symptoms of Depression

NIMH also lists several symptoms that a woman who is depressed may experience. Not every woman who is depressed will experience everything listed. Also, the severity of symptoms varies with individuals and also varies over time. Here are some symptoms:

* Persistent sad, anxious, or "empty" mood

* Feelings of hopelessness, pessimism

* Feelings of guilt, worthlessness, helplessness

* Loss of interest or pleasure in hobbies and activities that were once enjoyed

* Decreased energy, fatigue, being "slowed down"

* Difficulty concentrating, remembering, making decisions

* Insomnia, early-morning awakening, or oversleeping

* Appetite and/or weight loss or overeating and weight gain

* Thoughts of death or suicide; suicide attempts

* Restlessness, irritability

❉ Persistent physical symptoms that do not respond to treatment, such as headaches, digestive disorders, and chronic pain

It is interesting to note that NIMH also records that women experience depression about twice as often as men. Many hormonal factors may contribute to the increased rate of depression in women, particularly menstrual cycle changes, pregnancy, miscarriage, postpartum periods, pre-menopause, and menopause. Many women also face additional stresses such as responsibilities both at work and home, single parenthood, and caring for children and aging parents. Many women are also particularly vulnerable after the birth of a baby. The hormonal and physical changes, as well as the added responsibility of a new life, can be factors that lead to postpartum depression. While transient "blues" are common in new mothers, a full-blown depressive episode is not a normal occurrence and requires active intervention. Treatment by a sympathetic physician and the family's emotional support for the new mother are prime considerations in aiding her to recover her physical and mental well-being and her ability to care for and enjoy the infant.

A Self-Rating Depression Scale

Any woman who answers "true" to a majority of the following statements is almost certainly depressed and should seek professional assistance before the depression worsens:

❉ I feel like crying more often now than I did a year ago.

❉ I feel blue and sad.

❉ I feel hopeless a good part of the time.

❉ I have lost a lot of my motivation.

❉ I have lost interest in things I once enjoyed.

❉ I have had thoughts recently that life is just not worth living.

❉ My sleep patterns have changed of late. I either I sleep too much or too little.

❉ I am losing my appetite.

❉ I am too irritable.

❉ I am anxious of late.

❉ I have less energy than usual.

❉ Morning is the worst part of the day.

❉ I find myself introspecting a lot.

❉ When I look at myself in the mirror, I appear to be sad.

❉ My self-concept is not very good.

❉ I worry much about the past.

❉ I have more physical symptoms (headaches, upset stomach, constipation, rapid heartbeat, etc.) than I did a year ago.

❉ I believe people have noticed that I do not function as well at my job as I did in the past.

List taken from *Happiness is a Choice*, by Frank Minirth, M.D. and Paul Meier, M.D.

I would recommend showing this above list to the woman you are discipling who you think might be struggling with depression, and then see what she says. If she considers many of the statements to be true of her, ask her to elaborate. For example, if she says that she seems to have less energy or that her sleep patterns have changed, ask her to talk about it.

One of the best things you can do is to listen to her and really understand what she is going through and feeling. These previous statements can serve as a springboard for the discipler and disciple to talk about what she feels and about the pain she experiences.

Helping Your Disciple Dealing With Depression

The most important thing you can do for a woman dealing with depression is to help her get an appropriate diagnosis and treatment. This may involve encouraging her to stay with treatment until symptoms begin to abate (several weeks), or to seek different treatment if no improvement occurs. On occasion it may require making an appointment and accompanying her to the doctor.

The second most important thing is to offer emotional support. This involves understanding, patience, affection, and encouragement. Engage her in conversation and listen carefully. Do not disparage feelings expressed, but point out realities and offer hope. Don't ignore remarks about suicide. Report them to the depressed person's therapist. Invite her for walks and to outings, the movies, and other activities. Encourage participation in some activities that once gave pleasure, such as hobbies, sports, religious or cultural activities, but do not push the depressed person to undertake too much too soon. Your disciple needs diversion and company, but too many demands can increase feelings of failure.

Do not accuse your disciple of faking illness or of laziness, or expect her "to snap out of it." Eventually, with treatment, most women do get better. Keep that in mind, and keep reassuring her that with time and help, she will feel better.

The previous section was adapted from the pamphlet Depression, distributed by The National Institute of Mental Health.

Additional Help

Helpful Books

Happiness is a Choice, Frank Minirth, M.D. and Paul Meier, M.D.

Unveiling Depression in Women, Archibald Hart, Ph.D. and Catherine Webber Hart, Ph.D.

Seeing in the Dark: Getting the Facts on Depression and Finding Hope Again, Gary Kinnaman and Richard Jacobs

Overcoming Depression (Victory Over the Darkness), Neil Anderson and Joanne Anderson

Healing for Damaged Emotions, David A. Seamands

Online Resources

www.focusonthefamily.com (Focus on the Family)

www.webmd.com (overview, signs and symptoms of depression)

www.nimh.nih.gov (National Institute of Mental Health — signs and symptoms, local services)

In Summary

As you disciple women, over time you will encounter some who are dealing with depression. We are not doctors or counselors, so the best thing we can do is help our disciples get the help they need. We can pray for them, encourage them to get help, and walk alongside them in this journey. We can be a real tool of God in their lives, helping give hope and praying for their complete recovery from the pain of depression.

 ISSUE #9

Sexually Transmitted Diseases: "Who's going to want me now?"

"My boyfriend Jason has always been the jealous type. He gets outraged when I even look at another guy. I don't understand why he gets like this; we have been together for almost a year now, and I always tell him how much I love him and don't want anyone else."

I was sitting outside with my friend Jennifer as she recounted an incident that had happened the night before.

"So last night I needed to go to the bathroom so I excused myself and headed for the ladies room," she continued. "Jason followed me and accused me of going to see another guy in the restaurant. I yelled at him and pointed in his face that he has got to stop this jealousy and trust me for once. At that point he grabbed my hand, bit my finger, and stormed out of the place and left me there.

I was in shock. I looked at her bandaged hand and her tear-filled eyes.

"Jennifer," I began, "I just don't understand why you stay with him. I mean, you are beautiful, smart, and funny. Any guy would be lucky to have you — why are you staying with someone who treats you so bad?"

"Well," Jennifer answered, "Because he has given me herpes, and I don't think anyone else will want me now, so I stay just to have someone…"

Sexually transmitted diseases are commonplace, both inside and outside the church. When your disciple is reeling from the first news of her STD or struggling through an outbreak or other ramifications of a disease, you will need to be able to talk with her about it frankly. Understanding the circumstances surrounding her contraction of the disease, and which STD she has, can be very helpful as you walk through this issue with her. This chapter includes some basic information about STDs and how to help your disciple see the future with hope, optimism, and trust in God.

First Response

When your disciple confides that she has a sexually transmitted disease, you need to tell her you are proud of her for telling you and that you know that was not easy for her to do. Tell her you feel honored that she trusted you with that information and that you will not share it with anyone else. Ask her if she would like to share the details surrounding the contraction of the disease. If she doesn't feel comfortable telling you that at this time, ask her how else you can help.

In Over Your Head

You may feel inadequate to talk about this subject with your disciple if you do not know very much about STDs. It is okay to just ask questions, letting your disciple know you are going to help in any way possible and that you will do some research to better educate you and her both (if needed). Sometimes the way an STD was contracted may call for professional counseling. For example, if the woman was raped, contracted it from her husband who was having an affair, or faces one of any number of other situations, she may be dealing with some very deep pain. One woman I discipled had premarital sex with a boyfriend in high school, and years later found out she contracted an STD from him.

General Sexually Transmitted Disease Information

STDs are diseases you get by having intimate sexual contact — that is, having sex (vaginal, oral, or anal intercourse) with someone who already has the disease. Every year, STDs affect more than 13 million people.

According to www.epigee.org, "STDs, or STIs (for sexually transmitted infections) are infections that can be transferred from one person to another through sexual contact. According to the Centers for Disease Control and Prevention, there are over 15 million cases of sexually transmitted disease cases reported annually in the United States. Adolescents and young adults (15-24) are the age group at greatest risk for acquiring an STD, with 3 million becoming infected each year." The most common STDs include chlamydia, gonorrhea, hepatitis B, herpes, HIV/AIDS, human papilloma virus, syphilis, and candidiasis.

There are two different categories of STDs. One group is caused by bacteria and the other by viruses. STDs caused by bacteria can be treated and often cured with antibiotics. Some bacterial STDs include chlamydia, gonorrhea, trichomoniasis, and syphilis. STDs caused by viruses can be controlled, but not cured. If you get a viral STD, you will always have it. Some viral STDs include HIV/AIDS, genital herpes, genital warts, human papilloma virus (HPV), hepatitis B, and cytomegalovirus.

The symptoms vary among the different types of STDs. Some examples of common symptoms include unusual discharges from the vagina, sores or warts on the genital area, burning while urinating, itching and redness in the genital area, anal itching, soreness, or bleeding. Some STDs do not have symptoms, so it is imperative that a woman who has had sex get an examination.

Loving Her Through It

Whether your disciple is reeling from the news of an STD, or now has an STD and is in the process of clearing it up or managing it, we need to love her through the process. A couple of ways you can support her through this is by becoming educated with her about her STD and going with her to a doctor's appointment if she is scared or embarrassed. For certain, let her know you are sorry that this has happened and pray for her. I had a friend who contracted an STD, and it was awful for her. She was in excruciating pain and emotionally worn out. I prayed with her and for her to be healed and to not have any more outbreaks. This will be a devastating and embarrassing thing for your disciple — shower her with love, encouragement, and prayer.

Helpful Resources

It's one thing to sit in a high school class and learn about STDs. It's very different when your disciple has just gotten an abnormal report from the doctor and has found out she has one! If she comes to you for help, I hope this chapter gives you a few tracks to run on. For further information, you may want to visit some of these websites:

Epigee Women's Health: www.epigee.org (women's health, STDs)

National Institute of Child Health and Human Development: www.nichd. nih.gov/health/topics/sexually_transmitted_diseases.cfm

Center for Disease Control: www.cdc.gov/std/healthcomm/fact_sheets. htm (lists each disease and includes extensive facts, Q&A's, risks, complications, treatment options, etc., for each disease)

In Summary

If you haven't already, you will eventually disciple someone with an STD and will need to be ready to give her hope and encouragement as she deals with it. We need to have a basic understanding of STDs and be quick to offer our help and a shoulder to cry on. Reminding your disciple that all is not lost and that God can and will still do incredible things through her will be important for her in coping with the disease.

 **PART III**

Commonly Asked Questions

Here I've answered some of the questions I've received throughout the years about discipleship and related issues. I hope you find the answers you need.

1. "A woman asked me to disciple her, but what if I hardly know her?"

You might say to her, "I am so glad you have a desire to be discipled. One of the things I have found works best is for a person to get involved in one of our Bible study groups through church (or any other gathering). That way we can get to know each other. After a few months (or any length of time), we can talk more about beginning a discipleship relationship."

The bottom line here is that there is only one of you and (in some cases) many women who want to be discipled. You will not be able to physically disciple every woman who asks. While she gets involved in your church or group, you can better determine if you have the time and availability to disciple her. It will also give you time to determine if she has the qualities described in Chapter 3, "S.T.A.R.T. Discipling". Furthermore, if you don't have the time or availability, maybe another woman will surface who could disciple this woman and might even be a better match.

2. "How many people should I disciple at a time?"

It depends on how much time you have and what stage of life you're in. For example, if you are a single mom, you probably only have time for one disciple. But if your kids are in high school or college, you may have more time and could possibly disciple three or more. If you're in college with a full class load and a part-time job, you might only be able to disciple one person. But if it's your senior year and you're only taking a few classes, you might be able to take a couple more. So it really depends on how much time you have in your schedule. Remember, the appointments will last approximately one to two hours, and you'll also want extra time just to spend time together.

3. "What about group discipleship?"

You can disciple people together. I've found that if you are going to group-disciple people, it is best if they are at the same spiritual and maturity level. If not, the things you teach could be too deep for some and too basic for others. I don't disciple more than three at one time, and usually try to stick with two. This can be a great way to disciple women, as it adds more accountability, and when you need to miss a discipleship time, they can still get together without you.

4. "Where do I find women to disciple?"

If you'd like to begin to disciple a woman, look to the women around you at work, the gym, your neighborhood, and your church who are new believers or young in their faith. Build relationships with them and ask if they would like to get together to study the Bible and grow in their walk with God.

My friend Dawn was walking into her church one morning, and as she did so, she introduced herself to a woman who said she has just become a Christian six months before. As Dawn got to know this woman, she found out that she had never really been helped in her walk with God and did not know how to deepen her new relationship with Christ. Dawn offered to get together with her regularly, and thus began a discipleship relationship.

5. "Can I disciple someone of the opposite sex?"

I don't recommend discipling someone of the opposite sex for a variety of reasons. One, it hinders real self-disclosure. It's difficult for a man to tell a woman that he is struggling with lustful thoughts or pornography, and it's difficult for a woman to confess to a man that she's throwing up her food and doesn't like her body. These issues are best handled by a person of the same sex, who can better understand the issues and speak with empathy. Deep sharing of real-life issues and struggles is best disclosed between the same sex.

6. "How do I deal with burnout?"

Consider a Styrofoam cup filled with water. If you take a toothpick and punch a small hole in the side of the cup about a half-inch from the bottom, a little bit of water will slowly begin to seep out. If you continue to put water in the cup you can offset the small leak. However, if you poke about five small holes in the side of the cup without offsetting that leak with a consistent flow back into the cup, it will eventually become empty. Can you see where I'm going with this?

Take note of the things in your life that might be small drains. You have them; everybody does. They may take on the form of money issues, stressful relationships, demanding friends, or a child not walking with God. Then evaluate the things that "fill" your cup. These may be activities you enjoy, such as exercising, conversing with good friends, growing in your walk with God, or discipling a new believer. One thing I've found helpful in determining burnout is to make sure I'm constantly filling my cup and minimizing the drains. We can't totally eradicate the drains in this life, but we can make choices to minimize them. We can also embrace the fact that God won't burden us with things that we can't handle. When I feel burned out, I can usually attribute the drainage in my cup to lack of sleep, situations where I'm carrying burdens, or having said yes to too many things. Give your burdens to Jesus and ask Him to fill your cup anew.

7. "My disciple will not forgive people who have hurt her. What do I do?"

Few issues can stunt a woman's growth in the Lord like unforgiveness. Whether she is unforgiving of a dad who left her and her mother for another woman, a boyfriend who broke her heart, a husband who had an affair, or a dear friend who betrayed her, she needs to come to the point of forgiveness for her own sake and walk with God.

I would recommend Seven Steps to Freedom by Neil Anderson. It has helped me tremendously in my own forgiveness issues. There is a specific lesson on forgiveness that teaches that forgiveness is a choice you make, you will never feel like forgiving someone, and forgiveness is choosing to live with the consequences of another person's sin. I also recommend studying the issue of forgiveness in depth with your disciple from Scripture. Both of you can spend time together looking up passages throughout the Bible that deal with forgiveness, and then talk about how you can apply that Scripture to your lives. You could start with Scriptures such as Matthew 6:14-15 and 18:21-35, and Mark 11:25.

8. "Can I use the same material for each woman I disciple?"

If you disciple women in a group and they are at the same level spiritually, then go ahead and use the same material for the group time. If you disciple women at different times during the week and they are also at the same level spiritually, then go ahead and use the same material as well. This will help you save time preparing each week. If the women you disciple are at different levels spiritually (i.e., one is a new believer and the other has been a Christian for a while and even leads her own Bible study or disciples others), you will need to use different material, as they are at such different places in their walk with God that either the material will be too basic for the more mature one or too complicated for the newer one.

9. "My disciple is sexually active — what should I say to her?"

On my website, www.lorijoiner.com, I have included a five-page Bible study that addresses this issue. Called "Standing Strong," it is a compilation of several different articles and worksheets I have come across during my years in ministry. It includes a section where your disciple can list the things she desires in a mate as well as create common-sense boundaries for maintaining sexual purity until marriage. Regardless of whether your disciple is sexually active or not, this Bible study is good material to cover together. Encourage her to let God's Word be her guide, not the world and its sexually charged ways. The study addresses what the Bible has to say about sex, lust, etc. It also has a section that describes God's purpose, plan, and provision for sex, as well as a section on starting over, forgiving ourselves and asking forgiveness where we have failed.

10. "What are some suggestions for spending time with my disciple?"

Think though your areas of interest as well as hers, and join each other in those activities. For example, does your disciple love to go to garage sales on Saturday mornings? Consider joining her one Saturday. Do you love to scrapbook? Perhaps you could go to a "crop" together. Other ideas include a play group with your kids, service in your church or community together, working out, study, playing tennis, running errands, Christmas shopping, taking a vacation, watching a movie, grabbing coffee and flipping through magazines, eating meals together, training for a road race together, or pampering yourselves with manicures or pedicures.

11. "How do I encourage my disciple to pray out loud?"

I would start by asking you disciple why she does not feel comfortable praying out loud. Reassure her that God sees our heart and is not concerned with our words as much as he is with the attitude of our hearts. Explain to her that prayer is just talking with God just as we would talk with a good friend. We don't have to use fancy words or eloquent speech. We just need to talk normally. Tell her she does not have to pray for a long time or any set amount of time. Encourage her to say a short prayer, just between you and her, for something easy — perhaps one thing she is thankful for. Also explain to her that one day she will be discipling others, and it will be very beneficial for them to see prayer modeled for their own understanding. So encourage her to pray with just the two of you to get started.

12. "What do I do if my disciple wears very revealing clothes?"

This is a delicate issue, as many women have different tastes, clothing styles, and body types, and I want to be sensitive to that. When I am just beginning to disciple a woman who is wearing very revealing clothes (i.e., her bra shows through her clothes, her thong is showing, part of her breasts show because her top is low-cut or too tight, her bottom shows when standing or sitting because of a skirt being too short), I do not bring this up. Instead, I take time to build the relationship, deepen trust, and show care for her. I want her to be absolutely confident that I am for her and on her side and want the best for her. If a woman confronts another woman about any issue (not just this one) without a caring relationship being built, hurt and bitterness can result, and the relationship can be damaged.

When a woman begins to grow in her relationship with God and to reach out to other women, disciple other women, or move into a position of leadership (in a ministry, in a church, etc.), then I begin to approach this subject with her. Since she is moving into a position of influence over and among other women, I take the step to have a conversation with her so she will be aware of how she is being perceived and can present herself differently so as to maintain a consistent witness for Christ.

I usually say something like this: "Hey Cassie, I wanted to chat with you today about something that is difficult for me to bring up. But because I care about you and want the best for you, I will bring it up. I have noticed that some of the clothes you wear are very revealing, and I was not sure you were aware of that and what others may think of you when you wear clothes that accentuate your chest (or behind, or whatever). When you dress in revealing (or super-tight) clothes, it sends a few messages I don't think you want to send. First, it sends a message that you are trying to get guys to look at the private parts of your body. It also sends a message of insecurity — as if guys would only notice you for your body instead of your beauty, your intelligence, and most of all your growing walk with God. Third, Christian men are our brothers in Christ. Many of them already struggle with lustful thoughts, and when we dress in sexually provocative ways, we only add to their struggle. Again, I hope you know how much I care about you, and I would not bring this up if I did not think it was best for you."

Oftentimes the woman I tell this to is hurt and defensive. That is okay — just remain calm, remind her that you are truly trying to help her and answer any questions she may have. You can stress that she does not have to dress like you — just that she may want to make a few different choices (i.e., layering low-cut shirts over another tank top that comes up higher on the chest, or double-checking a skirt length by sitting down and making sure it does not ride up the legs too far). Don't force her to comment or to say she will change. Just have the conversation and let her process it with the Lord and in her mind, and give her time to think about it.

I remember one woman I had this conversation with who was hurt at first. She closed down completely, and since I had saved this subject until the end of our time together, she left in that condition. However, she later thanked me profusely. She is now an incredible leader in her church, in teaching roles and among women in general. I am certain this would not be the case if she were still dressing the way she was.

It is human nature to make a quick judgment about people based on appearance, before they even open their mouths. As followers of Christ and witnesses for him, we sometimes need to make clothing choices that will help spread His gospel and not confuse it. Hang in there — I know this is a tough one!

13. "How do I set good boundaries with my disciples?"

There have been times throughout the years when as I start to disciple a woman, she begins to overwhelm me with constant phone calls, emails, and desires to be together often and at length. There is a problem with this on many different levels. One, your disciple needs to not depend on you for all her emotional, spiritual, and social needs. She needs to be connected to a larger body of believers besides you. Second, at different stages of life we will not have as much time as during others. For example, maybe you are finishing up your master's degree at a nearby seminary or are working two jobs to pay off some debt, so you don't have as much free time as you would like. Another example is if you are married and possibly have a few children, meaning your husband and children need to be your first priority. If you are neglecting them because of this one disciple's overwhelming needs (or you are discipling too many women), you need to reprioritize and make some needed adjustments.

You need to have a conversation with your disciple that may look something like this: "Karen, I enjoy getting together for our weekly times for discipleship, and it was a blast hanging out with you this past week at the park while our kids played on the playground. I am proud of you for the way you are growing in your faith in Christ. On my end, I need to make a few adjustments and reprioritize my husband and kids so that they don't feel neglected, and this is going to affect how much time we are able to spend together. I would like for you to get involved with a home group so you can meet some more women to hang out with when I am not available and for you to have others to talk to when I might be tied up with the kids. This does not affect our scheduled time together, and I will still be able to hang out periodically, but I need to spend more time with my family right now and just want to let you know this so you do not think I am avoiding you when I can't get together as much."

14. "The woman I was discipling quit — now what?"

Many times throughout my years of discipling women, there have been times when, for one reason or another, my disciple stops the relationship. There are a number of reasons for this. One, she may be too overwhelmed and busy in her life and not feel like she has the time to be discipled regularly. Two, she may be involved in some form of sin and does not want to quit that sin, and therefore does not want to be in a discipleship relationship where she would be challenged to change. Three, she may have gotten involved in another church or Christian organization and may want to be discipled in that group. I have had all three happen!

One thing to remember is to avoid beating yourself up over this. It is okay to evaluate if there is something you could have done differently. Maybe you could have prepared better, spent more time with the woman, etc. But I have found that this is going to happen and we need to rely on God. Trust that He will use the time you invested in her and the things you taught her at some point in her life down the line. Rely on God that He is in control of her growth, not you, and you need to trust his plan for her life. Reassure the woman that you hope for the best for her, you will pray for her, and that if she ever wants to start up again that you would love to continue.

15. "I'm discipling too many women — what now?"

If you have bitten off more than you can chew, or circumstances have changed in your life and you don't have the time to meet with all the women you are already discipling, I would recommend a few courses of action. First, consider grouping the women together. See what your schedule will allow and ask the women if they can all meet together at that time. Second, you could ask them to meet together without you for a season to pray together and study together (maybe a guided workbook with videos). Third, if one of the women you are discipling is mature in her faith, ask her to begin to disciple one of the newer women you are meeting with. You will just need to explain the position you are in to the women you are discipling and ask them if any of the above options would be a good fit for them.

16. "My disciple is heartbroken. How do I respond?"

When a woman is brokenhearted, regardless of age, it can be devastating. Beyond the shattered dream of love and security, she must deal with many other related dreams —planning a wedding, hopes of a family, growing old together, etc. The comfort and biblical encouragement you offer your disciple struggling with a broken heart will help her heal from the hurt, pain, and bitterness, and trust God with her future. Two books I have found extremely helpful in my own past brokenheartedness are *Shattered Dreams* by Larry Crabb and *Prayer Guide for the Broken Hearted* by Michelle McKinney-Hammond.

17. "What is accountability and how do I do this in discipleship?"

When a woman wants to walk out of any type of addiction, habit, or pattern in her life, she will need regular, encouraging accountability. When she wants to improve in an area such as Scripture memory, physical fitness, or time with God, she will be encouraged by regular accountability. After she presents an area to you, pray for her, ask her about that area regularly, and offer any godly and practical advice along the way to her attain her goal. Holding her accountable to her own goals will enable her to better achieve victory, and to continue victorious in any area of life. Just ask your disciple what area of life she is currently working on (purity in her thoughts, Scripture memory, not gossiping, etc.) and ask her what she would like to see different in that area. Then let her know you will pray for her in this area and that you will ask her about this area the next time you two meet. This is helpful because when she is tempted, let's say in the area of gossip, she will remember that you are going to ask her if she has done any better in that area and therefore she may rethink what she is about to say. One further note is that it is always beneficial for you as the discipler to lead the way in accountability, meaning you initiate sharing an area you are working on, and you both work through issues together.

18. "My disciple is viewing pornography regularly. How do I help her?"

If your disciple has shared this struggle with you, it seems to me that she wants help to stop the addiction. Let her know you are proud of her for telling you and that you know it takes courage to admit this struggle. Tell her you are in her corner and desire her to be victorious in this area. Next, ask her questions about what type of pornography (print, movies, and/or online) she views, what usually triggers the desire or urge to view the material, when she views it, how she usually feels afterward, how she thinks it is affecting her relationship with God, and how she thinks you can help. You could also ask if she has told others of this struggle or if she has sought any other help.

At this point you need to help her make some tough decisions. For example, if she is viewing online pornography, she may need to move her computer out into the living room and only turn it on when others are present. If her weakness comes at night, she may need to give the power cord to someone at a predetermined time each evening. If her struggle is

TV, she most likely needs to get rid of all cable channels and go back to just the basic channels (or give the TV away).

These suggestions are only outward helps, though. They make it harder to fill the desire when she is feeling tempted, which can be helpful, but the bigger issue is in the heart. She needs to deal with her heart and ask the Holy Spirit to fill her and enable her to say no to the temptation. What is driving this desire? That root needs to be uncovered and given to the Lord. Professional counseling may be needed. This is not an area to be taken lightly. It must be radically stopped, as the longer a woman is in it, the harder it becomes to stop.

Other resources that could be very beneficial are:

www.covenanteyes.com — This website offers a program that is loaded on your disciples' computer, and whatever sites she looks at are recorded for others to see. It is a great form of accountability. She can choose who can see the data.

www.lflforwomen.org — Lust Free Living is the company that owns this site. It offers a great resource that you as the discipler can use one-on-one or in a group of all women. It deals with lust as the core issue and problem instead of just merely dealing with the outward manifestations of lust such as pornography addictions, illicit sex, and frequent masturbation.

19. "Where do I find time to disciple when I have kids?"

There are several ideas to help find time disciple another woman when either (or both) of you have children. Perhaps you could find time to meet while your children are at school or preschool, after their bedtimes, while they nap, while the husbands watch them, by trading off paying for baby sitters, or while children watch a movie. One summer I discipled a single mom with two young girls. To serve her and her children, I taught the girls how to swim while she got some very needed time to herself. After the swim lesson we would eat a quick lunch, then they went down for a nap, which is when she and I began our discipleship time. For two years I discipled a high school girl while my children took afternoon naps.

Visit www.lorijoiner.com to download additional resources about Discipling Women such as:

* How to write a personal testimony

* Standing Strong Bible Study about sexual purity

* About your disciple — a get to know you worksheet

* Discipleship Evaluation — evaluating your discipleship ministry

* Answering objections and questions